THE CONSTITUTION, CONSENT AND COMMUNISM

A modern discussion on Constitutional originalism and how socialism is illegal under our Constitution

A CITIZEN ON THE
CONSTITUTION,
CONSENT AND COMMUNISM

*A Modern Discussion about Constitutional
Originalism and how Socialism is Illegal
Under our Constitution*

COLIN MCWAY

XULON PRESS

Liberty Hill Press
2301 Lucien Way #415
Maitland, FL 32751
407.339.4217
www.libertyhillpublishing.com

Unless otherwise indicated, Scripture quotations taken from (Version(s) used)

Printed in the United States of America.

ISBN-13: 978-1-5456-7624-0

ACKNOWLEDGEMENTS

This book, as I imagine with all books is the culmination of varied inspiration, encouragement and assistance. In my case those providing that support range from historical figures who I never met, to long-time friends and family and new friends who have lent a hand.

Of those historical figures who most influenced this book, James Madison has been most prominent. The combination of Madison's raw contribution to the founding of this nation along with the voluminous legacy he left through his writings that make clear the intent of our Constitution.

Second to Madison is Thomas Jefferson who so perfectly captured the essence of America in his Declaration of Independence. Without Jefferson's work it is hard to imagine what our Constitution would look like as the two are inextricably linked, with the Constitution enshrining Jefferson's eternal truths.

Less great than Madison and Jefferson, but still great, is Mark Levin who I believe serves as the country's most effective voice for our American principles.

I would be remiss if I did not include my most influential teacher, Anne Marie Ward of East Catholic High School in Manchester CT.

Although I was far from a good student Mrs. Ward recognized my love of history and encouraged me to pursue it in whatever fashion I desired.

There have been many who encouraged me along the way while wring this book, but several took the time to read and provide valuable feedback. Rob Wright, Tom Berger, and Joe Denny to name a few who took the time and energy to help steer the work. Mike Haridopolos provided much needed encouragement early in the process that the endeavor was a worthwhile one. Ron Brooks' help finding important outlets for the message is appreciated as well. As always in my business career Aline (Leener) Dwyer made my efforts look better than they are. Many others were gracious in listening to me while thinking through the arguments that I would use in the book, to them, sorry, and thank you.

The single biggest contributor however, has been my wife Suzanne without whom this book would not exist. Suzanne's initial impetuous was less out of a desire to for the book per se, instead it was more borne from her desire for me to stop screaming at the television; as in 'stop screaming at the television, why don't you write a book'! Once the project was started she patiently listened and help me form simple arguments with which to make my point. My retort when talking to friends of 'as I discuss in my upcoming book' has provided at least a couple of amusing tongue-in-cheek moments for us.

To all mentioned, and those not mentioned but provided encouragement, thank you.

TABLE OF CONTENTS

INTRODUCTION:

SO WHY THE BOOK? THE UNAMBIGUOUS FOUNDATION OF AMERICA

W e Americans have been blessed with the most humane form of government known in the history of mankind. Our governmental structure has created a society where the individual is the sovereign, where your talents, your energy, and your efforts are the determining factors in the success of your pursuit of happiness. However, the extraordinary freedoms with which we are blessed (and they are exceptional as history shows us) are rapidly eroding right in front of us. In many ways, we have already lost our republic. Who is to blame for our emersion into this totalitarian utopia? We are. Well, some of us are, many patriots have not taken our Republic for granted and have educated themselves on precisely what our founders have given us. I refuse to believe that Washington D.C. could get away with its unlawful behavior if the majority of the people truly knew the rules of the Republic. I am doing my small part to bring some more of my fellow citizens into the light.

This book's purpose is to articulate, in an accessible way, the continued relevance of how our republic came to be. I will demonstrate how our uniquely American governmental structure resulted from the founder's vision for a new world as a way to guard against the types of abuses they experienced under British rule. There are many excellent books on the subject of our founding process and principles, so while I feel the need to describe the process of our founding what I will demonstrate is that the context of the founding is necessary to understand how central those principles were to the founding process and how those principles remained central to our government for the next 150 years.

If I do my job, I believe that you will come to the conclusion that I have, that the only intellectually honest argument possible is for an originalist view of the Constitution and that those who want to think of the Constitution as either "living and breathing" or as outdated and irrelevant only do so because of the high hurdles the Constitution put in place to uphold our founding principles, barriers that serve to impede the reckless intent of the anti-constitutionalist. I will first take you through the founding process then once we have established our "more perfect union" I will begin to make a case for Constitutional originalism both through the document itself and by demonstrating with more current events how we are letting our republic slip away. I will stay almost entirely away from Constitutional law as I believe the Constitution itself is the precedent and not what an activist judge may rule.

I will keep this book as concise as possible as you should not need thousands of pages over several volumes to describe the intent of an original document that is only four pages long and a Bill of Rights whose ten amendments are each just one sentence. As was said in Shakespeare's Hamlet, "Brevity is the soul of wit." The brevity and wit that the framers have provided us resulted in the only government in the history of mankind borne of state's desires to enshrine and recognize the God-given, unalienable, natural rights of which citizens were already in possession.

Ben Franklin famously said when asked in 1787 at the Constitutional Convention "Well, Doctor, what have we got, a republic or a monarchy?" Franklin quickly responded, "A republic, if you can keep it." [1] I certainly believe that Franklin would agree that the key to keeping our Republic is understanding what it is in the first place.

So why are these foundational documents still relevant and crucial today? I won't go through a blow by blow of every aspect of the documents; instead, I'll focus on their origins and demonstrate the absolute consistency of their structure and the indelible mark of our founding principles on each. I will sometimes use quotes from our founders and other times, use the issues of today to prove my point. I do, however, encourage you to immerse yourself in the original sources as there is much more to the subject than one book, with a limited and specific purpose can accomplish.

I will conclude by doing an analysis of the tenets of communism both from Marx himself and as those principles are applied by political figures of today. My intent is to show that the principles of Marxism (or socialism, etc.) are both purposefully creeping into our society and that those principles are utterly incompatible with the founding principles of our republic and that they are wholly unconstitutional.

CHAPTER ONE
A LITTLE ABOUT ME

I am not one of the self-proclaimed "elite." I didn't graduate from Harvard. I didn't graduate from any college. I barely got out of high school. So who am I to write a book on the United States Constitution? Well, while I may not have been the world's best student, I did go on to hold leadership positions with several high-technology companies with a focus on first responder communications. I have long been fascinated with history and etymology (the study of word origins) and have been blessed with a curiosity of why things are the way they are. In many ways, I am the person that Madison, Hamilton, and Jay were speaking to when they published their 85 essays that became the Federalist Papers in their effort to convince the American people of the necessity for a more perfect Union. I believe the fact that I am not one of the "elite" is precisely the point. I don't believe in the *notion* of an elite, I believe in America's two overarching founding principles that were articulated in the Declaration of Independence that *all men are created equal* and that legitimate government can only exist with *the consent of the governed*. The idea of an elite class contradicts the principles of our American experiment. . This concept of an "elite" class is traceable to the progressive era that started in the early twentieth century where "educated" unelected bureaucrats believed they could and should solve all of the nation's woes through government and force their "solutions" upon the people without their consent. Since that time these elites have increasingly worked to marginalize the Constitution and to distance the people from it. We the people have been purposefully misled by these "elites" as they divide the nation and guide it off course while attempting to marginalize those who are opposed to their schemes.

I have always been interested in American history. When I was a 10-year-old boy I can remember dressing up as a minuteman with my cowboy hat pinned up on three sides to make a tricorne and tucking my pant legs into my socks to simulate breeches and kneesocks and I still remember being disappointed that my toy musket was a period incorrect percussion cap and not a flintlock. (I also ironed GI Joe's Marine Dress Blue Uniform, (oh, boy!) In my youth, my interest had always focused more on American military history and less on our unique political philosophy. My political philosophy evolved from that of an idealistic "social liberal" in my teens to more of a libertarian in my young adulthood to an educated Constitutional conservative in middle age. The evolution of my political philosophy was accompanied by much self-education, starting in earnest after the 2008 election of Barrack Obama when a friend gave me a copy of Mark R. Levin's book *Liberty and Tyranny*. The book was an eye-opener and put me on a course to discover everything I could about our unique American political philosophy.

My journey into American civics began with reading copies of the Declaration of independence and the United States Constitution that I had at my home (yes, hard copies), I was amazed at their simplicity. Why is it that we are taught, told and indoctrinated by the talking head "elites" in the media that these are outdated, complex, indecipherable documents and that you would need a "time machine" to be able to understand our Founding Fathers' intent? What I discovered was that the Constitution is only four pages long

2

and the Declaration is just one page (albethey large ones); the talk about complexity could not be farther from what I experienced. I wanted to really "own the material" contained in those documents so for three months I read them in whole or in part each day. It became apparent to me that while the Declaration of Independence has no traditional legal "standing" it is inextricably linked to the United States Constitution as the Declaration outlines our over-arching American principles while the Constitution serves as the legal framework in which those American principles are enshrined; principles for which we were willing to fight a revolution against the world's most powerful empire to gain the opportunity to form our own uniquely American society.

In America, our federal, central government had constitutional lim-itations placed upon it through a system of checks and balances and a clear delineation of jurisdiction; or at least that is how it is supposed to work. Today checks and balances, are needed on the self-proclaimed elite, be they elected or unelected. The best check that I can think of is a constitutionally literate citizenry who are willing and able to call out governmental overreach.

The United States of America has become a dangerously divided society. There are often calls to unite, but around what should we unite? Well, what brought the nation together, and indeed into exis-tence in the first place? If the United States needs to *unite* around something, I think that *thing* is our Constitution and our founding principles, if not that, then what could we possibly rally around?

In this book, I won't refer to Democrats or Republicans as those terms are increasingly meaningless. Instead, I see the world in unambiguous terms, one is either a Constitution originalist or one is an anti-Constitutionalist. You will see that there is not a whole lot of necessity for *interpreting* the Constitution as the intent, language, and structure of our founding documents is plain. Once an individual moves beyond the obvious original intent and tries to have black mean white, you become an anti-constitutionalist. This is not to say that there can't be some deviation in thought. For example, the Fourth Amendment refers to "reasonable" search and seizure, and the Eighth amendment to "excessive" fines we can debate what is and what is not reasonable or excessive. But we can't say that choosing to not participate in commerce is participating in commerce.

I hope to show how simple, powerful and consistent the ideas of our founding are and that once those principles were enshrined in the Constitution nothing has systemically undone them, our government has simply become unmoored to those principles. I will continually demonstrate the importance of two of these ideas. Once we thoroughly understand how central these ideas are to our founding, you will then be able to clearly see when the anti-constitutionalist is trying to lead us further astray.

The two most powerful ideas of our founding are:

1. *All men are created equal.* I will demonstrate how this simple yet powerful idea runs through most of our early history. This concept, contrary to what you may hear or read makes our founding one that sees no race, sex, religion, or any of the other groups the anti-constitutionalist tries to claim the Constitution discriminates against. You will also see how this idea is related to unalienable rights and the freedom of religion.
2. *The Consent of the governed.* I will demonstrate how, through every step of our founding, the central government asked the states for permission to take over logical, discreet, and finite

functions. The central government committed to the states that they would only make laws pertaining to those agreed to functions. The states warily agreed to those unambiguous terms. Then, one day, that process stopped, the central government just stopped asking for permission to control ever-increasing aspects of our society, but they kept taking. They no longer have our consent.

America is its Constitution, it is simple, clear, finite, and consented to. Constitution originalists can point to where their principles come from, they can point to the limits that have been placed upon the government, and they can describe the process by which they will abide if they wish to change the government's role in society. The anti-constitutionalist can do no such thing. The anti-constitutionalist disparages our past as a way to de-legitimatize the Constitution. The anti-constitutionalist believes he has no limits placed upon him, he does not think he needs your consent, and he will not tell you where he is trying to take you because he has no idea what end state he is trying to create. The only way to stop the anti-constitutionalist is to expose his recklessness.

CHAPTER 2.

GETTING TO INDEPENDENCE

~~~~~~~~~~~~~~~~~~~~~~~~~~~~~~~~~~~~~

L et's look first at our Declaration of Independence and the process by which we got to it. Understanding the Declaration of Independence is essential for understanding the Constitution. One could not possibly understand the Constitution absent the context provided by the Declaration, and with the context of the Declaration, the Constitution is impossible to misunderstand.

By the 1760s and 1770s, the American colonies had been subject to British rule for about 150 years, and the colonists were becoming increasingly displeased with the heavy-handed totalitarian rule of King George III. In grammar school, we learn about events such as "The Stamp Act," the "Boston Tea Party" and the "Boston Massacre" and other events that made the colonists understandably disenchanted with their rulers in London. Through these difficult times, most colonists still believed relations with the crown would improve. However, groups of patriots in various colonies began an active resistance to the crown. Entities with names like The Sons of Liberty, The Committees of Safety and the Committee of Correspondence effectively ran a shadow government, trained the militia's Minute Men and organized public support for the cause of liberty. Then on April 19th 1775 the British Regulars (I include the term regulars because we were all British at the time) under the command of General Thomas Gage, would attempt to quell the increasingly unruly colonials and seize their arms and supplies stored west of Boston in the town of Concord (although much of it had already been relocated to other towns). This did not go as planned for the regulars and it was an early lesson in what happens when you try to separate an American from his gun. Early that morning, 700 or so, regulars encounter 80 Minute Men in the town of Lexington, just to the east of Concord. In the confusion, a shot rings out, the famous "shot heard round the world," and the battle is joined. The battle swells and moves on to Concord, which temporarily falls, the regulars are eventually beaten back and harassed by colonial militia all the way back to Boston. While the battles of Lexington and Concord were not particularly large, it was now almost certain that there was to be no making amends with the crown; the colonies were now in a state of war with the most powerful empire in the world.

Shortly after the battles of Lexington and Concord the Second Continental Congress convenes in May of 1775. In July of 1775 the colonists make one last attempt at reconciliation with the crown. Further turmoil will transpire during the one year period from spring and summer of 1775 until the summer of 1776 including further bloodshed at Bunker Hill on June 17th, 1775, naval blockades of American ports and other escalations, the Second Continental Congress officially severs colonial ties with the British Empire on July 4th (or thereabouts) 1776 and Congress publishes the Declaration of Independence.

The process of creating the Declaration of Independence began, in earnest, one month prior to July 4th with the "Lee Resolution" when on June 7, 1776, upon the instructions of the Virginia delegation, Richard Henry Lee drafted for consideration by the Second

Continental Congress, in part, (the resolution also referenced treaties and forming a confederation of states) the following resolution:

Resolved, That these United Colonies are, and of right ought to be, free and independent States, that they are absolved from all allegiance to the British Crown, and that all political connection between them and the State of Great Britain is, and ought to be, totally dissolved[1].

Several days later on the 10th of June, in preparation for what Congress believed would be the eventual passage of the Lee Resolution, Congress formed the "Committee of Five" to begin drafting the Declaration of Independence as the methodology by which the colonies would announce their separation from Great Britain. As a point of clarification as it is not often discussed, first the Lee Resolution must pass a vote in the Second Continental Congress, the passage is then announced via the Declaration of Independence. The following day the 11th of June, John Adams of Massachusetts, Benjamin Franklin of Pennsylvania, Thomas Jefferson of Virginia, Robert Livingston of New York and Roger Sherman of Connecticut were named to the Committee of Five.

It fell upon Jefferson to draft the Declaration after Lee was appointed to the committee addressing confederation (and his wife fell ill) and Adams felt too unpopular for the task. Jefferson draws upon sources including his own work from a draft of the Virginia Declaration of Rights and the work of fellow Virginian George Mason from the same document. Two weeks later on June 28th, 1776 a draft of the Declaration is presented to Congress, then on July 2nd, 1776 the Lee Resolution is passed by Congress and on July the 5th the Declaration of Independence is published; it is signed by most signatories on August 2nd, 1776.

Let's look at it what our Declaration of Independence says and what I think it means. First is the Introduction it says:

IN CONGRESS, July 4, 1776.

The unanimous Declaration of the thirteen united States of America,

When in the Course of human events, it becomes necessary for one people to dissolve the political bands which have connected them with another, and to assume among the powers of the earth, the separate and equal station to which the Laws of Nature and of Nature's God entitle them, a decent respect to the opinions of mankind requires that they should declare the causes which impel them to the separation.[2]

This first sentence is usually referred to as the introduction. In the introduction, Jefferson simply says that sometimes countries split apart because the people within a country can no longer tolerate being mistreated by those in power. Jefferson further says the colonies are not subservient to the crown and that the colonies are intrinsically entitled to equal status with the crown. Jefferson goes on to articulate our rights and how the crown has violated those rights which, in turn, has led to the colonies declaring their independence.

A Note to the Non-Religious: Jefferson's reference to *Nature and Nature's God* is by no means advocacy for theocracy. Certainly not from Jefferson who was more skeptical of organized religion than many of the founders, although he was far from the atheist some claim, as atheists are not regular and consistent churchgoers as was Jefferson. Instead, Nature and Natures God contemplates the universality of unalienable Rights and that these rights cannot be given out by or be controlled by Man.

This next section is typically referred to as the preamble; it is magnificent.

We hold these truths to be self-evident, that all men are created equal, that they are endowed by their Creator with certain unalienable Rights, that among these are Life, Liberty and the pursuit of Happiness. That to secure these rights, Governments are instituted among Men, deriving their just powers from the consent of the governed, That whenever any Form of Government becomes destructive of these ends, it is the Right of the People to alter or to abolish it, and to institute new Government, laying its foundation on such principles and organizing its powers in such form, as to them shall seem most likely to effect their Safety and Happiness. Prudence, indeed, will dictate that Governments long established should not be changed for light and transient causes; and accordingly all experience hath shewn, that mankind are more disposed to suffer, while evils are sufferable, than to right themselves by abol-ishing the forms to which they are accustomed. But when a long train of abuses and usurpations, pursuing invariably the same Object evinces a design to reduce them under absolute Despotism, it is their right, it is their duty, to throw off such Government, and to provide new Guards for their future security. Such has been the patient sufferance of these Colonies; and such is now the necessity which constrains them to alter their former Systems of Government. The history of the present King of Great Britain is a history of repeated injuries and usurpations, all having in direct object the establishment of an absolute Tyranny over these States. To prove this, let Facts be submitted to a candid world.[3]

In the preamble, Jefferson defines what it means to be American; the preamble is the embodiment of the American spirit. Jefferson's phrase *"all men are created equal"* is genuinely and literally an extraordinarily revolutionary concept in 1776. I believe it is the most crucial concept in all of the American political formation.

In the 18th century, throughout Europe (and much of the world) monarchies, which etymologically means *alone to rule,* are the predominant form of government. Also in the 18th century, the "western world" is more much religiously oriented than are societies today. So what do the monarchs do? They declare that they are, in fact, ordained by God. Subjects, therefore, are not the equal of the monarch. This stance makes being against the Monarch equal to being against God, a very clever and evil way to grab and hold power. So, Jefferson is essentially saying to King George, 'you're no better than me.' I think it is difficult today to grasp the gravity of that statement at that time. The phrase *all men are created equal* lays the foundation for an American society based on meritocracy where you are free to utilize your talents and your effort to determine your own outcome, a society not reliant upon a class or caste system of predetermined outcomes. Importantly, Jefferson's use of the word equal means equal in the eyes of God and the law; not some entitlement to equal outcomes as that would require intervention by man. This natural equality simply recognizes our inalienable Right to pursue our own happiness.

Jefferson affirms that if we are the equal of the monarch, and unalienable Rights cannot possibly come from someone who is our equal, so where then do they come from? Obviously then, your actual Rights come from God, they are intrinsic and universal and do not stem from any government; that government can't give you any rights, and they can't take any Rights away. Remarkable. I believe the phrase also lays the groundwork for religious liberty and a society that is absent of a state-run church. Think of it this way, the monarch was also the "Supreme Governor" of the church (the monarch could not be the *Head of the Church*, biblically that role is Jesus'). It was the monarch's church, so if there is to be no monarch in America claiming divine appointment, then there can be no "state church" either. *All men are created equal;* simply the five most powerful words of political speech in the history of mankind.

Jefferson then moves to another extraordinary concept, affirming that legitimate government can only emanate from the *"consent of the governed"*. I find it so odd that today the "left" tries to lay claim to Jefferson as their own in their government-centric world. No one who espoused an idea such as *consent of the governed* would be supportive of an un-elected, unaccountable bureaucratic monstrosity such as we have in our current bloated administrative state. The *concept of consent of the governed* is not an original notion of Jefferson or the founders; instead, it was a principle that came out of the mid and late 17th century from political philosophers such as John Locke and others during the "Age of Reason" and "The Enlightenment." Locke's ideas had a tremendous influence on all of the founders. *Consent of the governed* in effect means 'you can only do to me what I say you can do to me'; making the case that the American government will necessarily be a limited one. It is impossible to consent to an unnamed, unelected bureaucrat because the bureaucrat never even asks for consent. *Consent of the governed,* like *all men are created equal* was radical at the time as it too rejected the previously unbreakable grip that a Monarchy held over its subjects. Jefferson goes on to make the point that while throwing off the government is not a frivolous act, society has the God-given, unalienable Right to do so if the people no longer consent to that government. Jefferson also explains that we must have reached a dire point in the summer of 1776 because societies are much more likely to complain about malfeasances than they are to remedy them.

Finally, Jefferson summarizes saying in effect that 'we are now at that intolerable point and I will lay out the case with a delineation of our grievances.

1. *He has refused his Assent to Laws, the most wholesome and necessary for the public good.*

2. *He has forbidden his Governors to pass Laws of immediate and pressing importance unless suspended in their operation till his Assent should be obtained; and when so suspended, he has utterly neglected to attend to them.*

3. *He has refused to pass other Laws for the accommodation of large districts of people unless those people would relinquish the right of Representation in the Legislature, a right inestimable to them and formidable to tyrants only.*

4. *He has called together legislative bodies at places unusual, uncomfortable, and distant from the depository of their public Records, for the sole purpose of fatiguing them into compliance with his measures. He has dissolved Representative Houses repeatedly, for opposing with manly firmness his invasions on the rights of the people.*

5. *He has refused for a long time, after such dissolutions, to cause others to be elected; whereby the Legislative powers, incapable of Annihilation, have returned to the People at large for their exercise; the State remaining in the mean time exposed to all the dangers of invasion from without, and convulsions within.*

6. *He has endeavoured to prevent the population of these States; for that purpose obstructing the Laws for Naturalization of Foreigners; refusing to pass others to encourage their migrations hither, and raising the conditions of new Appropriations of Lands.*

7.   He has obstructed the Administration of Justice, by refusing his Assent to Laws for establishing Judiciary powers.

8.   He has made Judges dependent on his Will alone, for the tenure of their offices, and the amount and payment of their salaries.

9.   He has erected a multitude of New Offices, and sent hither swarms of Officers to harrass our people, and eat out their substance.

10. He has kept among us, in times of peace, Standing Armies without the Consent of our legislatures.

11. He has affected to render the Military independent of and superior to the Civil power.

12. He has combined with others to subject us to a jurisdiction foreign to our Constitution, and unacknowledged by our laws; giving his Assent to their Acts of pretended Legislation:

13. For Quartering large bodies of armed troops among us:

14. For protecting them, by a mock Trial, from punishment for any Murders which they should commit on the Inhabitants of these States:

15. For cutting off our Trade with all parts of the world:

16. For imposing Taxes on us without our Consent:

17. For depriving us in many cases, of the benefits of Trial by Jury:

18. For transporting us beyond Seas to be tried for pretended offences

19. *For abolishing the free System of English Laws in a neighbouring Province, establishing therein an Arbitrary government, and enlarging its Boundaries so as to render it at once an example and fit instrument for introducing the same absolute rule into these Colonies:*

20. *For taking away our Charters, abolishing our most valuable Laws, and altering fundamentally the Forms of our Governments:*

21. *For suspending our own Legislatures, and declaring themselves invested with power to legislate for us in all cases whatsoever.*

22. *He has abdicated Government here, by declaring us out of his Protection and waging War against us.*

23. *He has plundered our seas, ravaged our Coasts, burnt our towns, and destroyed the lives of our people.*

24. *He is at this time transporting large Armies of foreign Mercenaries to compleat the works of death, desolation and tyranny, already begun with circumstances of Cruelty & perfidy scarcely paralleled in the most barbarous ages, and totally unworthy the Head of a civilized nation.*

25. *He has constrained our fellow Citizens taken Captive on the high Seas to bear Arms against their Country, to become the executioners of their friends and Brethren, or to fall themselves by their Hands.*

26. *He has excited domestic insurrections amongst us, and has endeavoured to bring on the inhabitants of our frontiers, the*

merciless Indian Savages, whose known rule of warfare, is an undistinguished destruction of all ages, sexes and conditions.

In every stage of these Oppressions We have Petitioned for Redress in the most humble terms: Our repeated Petitions have been answered only by repeated injury. A Prince whose character is thus marked by every act which may define a Tyrant, is unfit to be the ruler of a free people.

Nor have We been wanting in attentions to our British brethren. We have warned them from time to time of attempts by their legislature to extend an unwarrantable jurisdiction over us. We have reminded them of the circumstances of our emigration and settlement here. We have appealed to their native justice and magnanimity, and we have conjured them by the ties of our common kindred to disavow these usurpations, which, would inevitably interrupt our connections and correspondence. They too have been deaf to the voice of justice and of consanguinity. We must, therefore, acquiesce in the necessity, which denounces our Separation, and hold them, as we hold the rest of mankind, Enemies in War, in Peace Friends.[4]

That's quite a list of our grievances. I process the list of grievances into four categories, all of which will later find their remedies in the Constitution.

The first category of grievances is around the principle of self-government. Before the Declaration of Independence, the colonies wanted to remain British subjects, but govern themselves. However, the crown was not interested in subjects who were self-governing, so they would dissolve legislatures, not approve laws passed by legislatures, make the legislative process burdensome by setting meetings at odd locales and times, and not ratify colonial courts. These actions made it all but impossible for the colonists to govern themselves, and the colonists believed, put the colonies at risk from both internal chaos and external threat.

The second category of grievances was the crown limiting the growth of the colonies by establishing both restrictive immigration policy and by implementing policies limiting geographic expansion. The colonists believed that the crown thought that if the colonies grow too large, they would be ungovernable, a bit ironic.

The third category of grievances is around the lack of separation of powers. The crown's courts were answerable to the king, so there was no independent colonial judiciary; the colonists were not necessarily entitled to a trial by jury, the accused were sometimes sent oversees for trials, the colonies were also beset with new bureaucracies without their consent and forced to pay for them.

The fourth category of grievances was the most egregious, and that was of military supremacy. While the first three categories are all tyrannical, I believe as Jefferson points out, that it takes a lot to make the society willing to throw off the government. Included within my category of military supremacy are actions such as, as the name of the category implies, placing the military above the civil authority, keeping a standing army, quartering troops in the homes of the colonists and making troops largely unaccountable for crimes. The military supremacy led to the crown waging active war on its own subjects, engaging foreign mercenaries and Indian tribes to do the same and kidnapping colonists and pressing them into service against their fellow countrymen.

After the exhaustive list of grievances, Jefferson also makes a point of saying that the colonies have tried to work with the crown on these issues and that this declaration is not their first attempt to bring to the crown's attention their state of dissatisfaction.

Jefferson then makes the Declaration itself where we see part of the original language of the Lee Resolution. We also see the incredible pledge to themselves and each other of their *Lives, our Fortunes, and our sacred Honor*. Everything was at stake.

We, therefore, the Representatives of the United States of America, in General Congress, Assembled, appealing to the Supreme Judge of the world for the rectitude of our intentions, do, in the Name, and by Authority of the good People of these Colonies, solemnly publish and declare, That these United Colonies are, and of Right ought to be Free and Independent States; that they are Absolved from all Allegiance to *the British Crown, and that all political connection between them and the State of Great Britain, is and ought to be totally dissolved; and that as Free and Independent States, they have full Power to levy War, conclude Peace, contract Alliances, establish Commerce, and to do all other Acts and Things which Independent States may of right do. And for the support of this Declaration, with a firm reliance on the protection of divine Providence, we mutually pledge to each other our Lives, our Fortunes and our sacred Honor*[5]

CHAPTER 3:

AN IMPERFECT UNION

The 13 colonies have now declared independence from Great Britain and are engaged in a war to secure that independence. Incidentally, the war is, in fact, a type of civil war, the difference between a civil war and a revolution is, simply, who the winner is. The war rages until the battle of Yorktown Virginia on October 19, 1781, it takes another two years for the Treaty of Paris to be signed on September 3, 1783. Almost 25,000 Americans are killed on the battlefield, die from their wounds or while being held, prisoner. The number of Americans killed represented about 5 percent of the fighting age, eligible men in the colonies.

During the period of the Revolutionary War, the Second Continental Congress was the only form of a central government. There wasn't a powerful executive or executive branch departments to conduct the innumerable tasks of running the war so that work was accomplished by Congress through various and numerous committees. At the time, the individual colonies viewed themselves as independent nation-states that had come together for the primary purpose of executing the war of independence, but it was becoming clear that some additional central authority would be beneficial while conducting the business of government during the war.

Even before the publication of the Declaration of Independence, Congress began addressing the issue. Within the original Lee Resolution of June 1776 was a recommendation for a plan to form a confederation of the states. It stated simply:

That a plan of confederation be prepared and transmitted to the respective Colonies for their consideration and approbation.[1]

A confederation is simply a loose federation. Congress developed a plan for a confederation and debated the resolution from July 1776 until the Articles of Confederation were finally approved by Congress in October 1777 and were submitted to the states for ratification. It took until March of 1781 for all of the states to ratify the Articles. Although not ratified until 1781 Congress, nonetheless, used the Articles as a framework to manage the war effort and conduct the business of the country. The limited central powers granted under the Articles of Confederation were essentially those powers that the states perceived would have been the legitimate, centralized role for the king and the Parliament on the continent.

The Articles of Confederation were a notoriously weak form of government, granting no central taxation power, eventually resulting in unpaid Revolutionary War debt. Under the Article's, Congress could only *request* funds from the states to pay these debts, the states seldom paid, and the states were also taxing one another. Additionally, the absence of a single executive to lead negotiations with other nations made it challenging to conduct foreign diplomacy and regulate foreign trade.

The weak government of the Articles of Confederation led to a near chaotic situation and made it increasingly clear to the states that changes were needed to the Articles. Shay's Rebellion around

Springfield, Massachusetts in 1786 and 1787 further hastened the call for changes. Shay's rebellion was an armed uprising stemming largely from the confiscation of the property of residents in rural areas of Massachusetts, who upon returning from the war borrowed money to start farms. Currency shortages and other issues caused many farmers to fall into delinquency and remedies sought at the state legislature and in the courts were unsuccessful. Thousands of disenchanted citizens armed and mobilized until a privately funded militia under Continental Army General Benjamin Lincoln succeeded in putting down the rebellion.

It is in this tumultuous atmosphere that an attempt to bolster the confederation's limited central authority was initiated by several of the States, (New Jersey, New York, Pennsylvania, Delaware, and Virginia) led in part by James Madison of Virginia gathered in Annapolis, Maryland in September of 1786 to address shortcomings of the Articles. The focus of the Annapolis Convention was primarily around trade, but it quickly became evident to the attendees that an effort broader in scope and participation was necessary. The convention's attendees unanimously voted to recommend that a Constitutional Convention be held with delegates from all of the States and that those delegates be granted authority broader than trade alone. This recommendation was contained in the Annapolis Convention's final report to Congress and sent to the States. Accepting the Annapolis Convention's suggestion, in February 1787 Congress authorizes a Constitutional Convention to be held the following May in Philadelphia.

OK, so all this is interesting, but so what? What I think is essential through this process is that whether it is before the revolution, during the revolution or afterward under the Articles of Confederation that the States all see themselves as independent, sovereign entities; not willing to give away that sovereignty to a central government and now as we move to the Constitutional Convention in Philadelphia, it will be the States that will give birth to the Federal government. I find it completely impossible to believe that the States, who all believed in their individual sovereignty, would cede their sovereignty in totality to an all-powerful central government. And in fact, they don't. The States do realize that there is a necessity for *some* more central authority, but not plenary powers or a national government.

Originally scheduled to begin on May 14, 1787, the start date of the Constitutional Convention needed to be pushed back until May 25 as only several attendees made their way to Philadelphia by the 14th. Travel in the late 18th century was even less convenient than it is today. James Madison was among the first to arrive, and soon the entire Virginia delegation made its way to Philadelphia. Madison and his colleagues used the period before the revised commencement date to draft the *Virginia Plan*. The Virginia Plan was used as a template to shape debate throughout the convention, contained within its 15 resolutions were prominent features such as a system of checks and balances including three branches of government, legislative, executive and judicial, a bicameral Congress and population-based proportioning of seats to be granted to each State. The Virginia Plan's resolutions contemplated an increase in scope for a central government that was successful in moving the convention beyond merely tinkering with the Articles of Confederation to forming a new and uniquely American form of government.

Some people say that the Constitutional convention was hijacked and therefore illegitimate, I say hooey. Broadening the scope of the convention was accepted by the delegates, who were themselves given authority to deal with the general flaws contained in the Articles. It was also fully recognized that the states would be required to ratify any work that came out of the convention. Moreover, even though the Articles of Confederation were a weak form of government with a mono-cameral structure many of the ideas contained in the articles made it to the Constitution, so I think a strong argument can be made that, by and large, the Articles were modified. Arguments to the contrary are disingenuous and made by people who need to nullify the Constitution to advance their own nefarious political ends. Theoretically, given the limited scope of the Annapolis Convention *it* could have been "hijacked," but instead of overstepping their predetermined bounds, the attendees of that convention requested a broader, more inclusive one that had as its purpose to remedy the bulk of the ills of the Articles of Confederation.

On May 25th, 1787 the Constitutional Convention goes into session, and George Washington is immediately elected to preside over the process. A policy of secrecy is instituted, no press is allowed, and the windows to the Pennsylvania State House are even reportedly nailed shut during the hot and humid Philadelphia summer. James Madison, who attended every session, transcribed the debate that took place over the 100 days of the Convention. Because of Madison's effort, we have a thorough understanding, albeit from one source, of the goings-on that hot summer in Philadelphia. Madison's notes to the Constitutional Convention are a 'must read' for anyone looking to gain further insight into the tenor of the sessions.

There were several main topics of discussion during the convention; however, most of the debate can be viewed as involving extreme skepticism about centralized governmental authority; the colonists had just thrown off a tyrant and had no intention of replacing one tyrant with another tyrant or with a tyrannical legislature. It is paramount to keep in mind that this federal government is being born of states who are themselves sovereign, they do however mainly recognize that the Articles are insufficient and are an ineffective form of government and that there is a necessity for some limited increase in the role of a central authority.

Before looking more deeply at the Constitution's seven articles that emerge at the end of the convention, I'll highlight a couple of the main topics the delegates debated to evidence both the colonists' distrust of centralized power and their requirement of continued primacy of the states. Determining representation in Congress was a challenging issue. The Virginia plan, also known as the *Large State Plan* because it proposed population-based determination of the number of seats each state would be granted. The small States were infuriated as they believed their states would cease to be relevant. This issue was debated for weeks, and at one point the issue almost entirely derailed the convention. In response to the Virginia Plan, the New Jersey delegation proposed a mono-cameral plan, known too as the Small State Plan, which would keep the one vote per state method as currently existed under the Article of Confederation. Now the more populous States are incensed. Roger Sherman and the Connecticut Delegation then put forward a plan melding the ideas in the Virginia and New Jersey plans. The Connecticut Compromise as it became known proposed a bicameral legislature with the lower house (House of Representatives) being proportional to population and an upper house (the Senate) where every State would receive two seats, to be appointed by the State legislatures. Initially, the Connecticut plan was also not looked upon favorably, but within a couple of weeks, it gained favor and was accepted.

Most of us, at least generally know this story, but today what is crucial to recognize as we bound blindly down the road to a *universal* federal government is that the States, giving birth to the federal government are insistent that the Congress be meaningfully reflective of the States and that the three branches of government that emerge are co-equal and that there is a system of checks and balances among them. In fact, the states are so integral to the structure of the new government through the apportionment of seats in the House of Representatives, the structure of the Senate and the required state approval of changes in the Constitution through the amendment process that I would argue that there were four branches of government, not three. If a national government was the desire, then they certainly would not have structured or limited government as they proceeded to do. As it pertains to the Congress, they could have simply had one house and national elections, or many other ways that would diminish the role of the states. In the structure of the Senate, state primacy is even more evident as the delegates agreed to have the same number of seats for each state because the states viewed themselves as equals. Furthermore, those Senate seats were to be selected by the state legislatures because the delegates wanted the interest of their sovereign states to be heard, not only the populous within the states. We will see much more of the limited role Congress is given when we look at the final product that the delegates produce.

The debate around the structure of the executive branch is one example of the many ways that the delegates attempted to check potential tyranny in the architecture of the Constitution. The debate around the structure of the Executive branch was focused on two primary issues, both in recognition of the fact they had just thrown off a tyrant. The delegates recognized the necessity of an executive who would generally implement, or execute the laws Congress passed. There was substantial debate regarding how the president would be appointed, one of the ideas turned down again, evidences the delegates' desire for separation of powers. The concept proposed was that the president would be voted on by Congress, but it was believed the president then would simply be a "creature of Congress." It was ultimately determined the president be elected by a system of electors chosen by the state legislatures, again recognizing the importance of the states. The powers of the executive were also debated; including that of veto power. It was understood that a veto is an essential check of Congress; however, the concern was around having one man be able to block justly passed legislation. The delegates came together around the idea of an override vote of 2/3rds by each house of Congress. Another contentious debate was around the term of the presidency. The delegates were keenly aware that without a term of office, a monarch or despot could emerge. The delegates again came together, agreeing to a four-year term for the presidency, but did not place a limitation on the number of terms the president could serve.

Several committees did the specific work of the convention, on September 8, 1787, William Samuel Johnson of Connecticut, Alexander Hamilton and Gouverneur Morris of New York, James Madison of Virginia, and Rufus King of Massachusetts are appointed to the Committee of Style. The Committee of Style, tasked with organizing the content based around the concept the delegates have agreed, presents a draft of the Constitution to the Convention. The various articles will contain the structure of the proposed branches of government and the powers and limits placed upon those branches. On September 12, 1787, a draft was presented to the convention. The debate takes place over the next several days, and the text is finally approved by the 39 remaining of the original 55 delegates and submitted to Congress. On September 17, 1787, Congress unanimously consents to the Constitution and adjourns, signaling that their work on the issue is finished (this is why we celebrate September 17th as Constitution day, even though it has not yet been ratified by the states) and then, two weeks later on September 28, 1787 Congress unanimously agrees to forward to the Constitution to the states where ratification conventions will be held.

The document that is forwarded to the states is a very concise document featuring just seven articles, one of which is simply a description of the one-time process for ratification of the Constitution. The original text is only four pages long (although the pages were about 28 by 20 inches). I think all citizens should be able to articulate, generally, the structure of the Constitution. I process its architecture like this:

There are seven articles
    Article One: describes the structure and role of the Legislature
    Article Two: describes the structure and role of the Executive
    Article Three: describes the structure and role of the Supreme Court
    Article Four: generally explains what the states should expect and how new states can be added

So the first four of the seven articles lay out the entire structure of the central government and the relationship between the federal government and the states. The next three articles, I think of as administrative or clarifying articles.

Article five: describes how Congress or the states can amend the Constitution
Article six: describes treaty powers and asserts supremacy on those powers granted to the central government and contains an overt requirement of an oath demanding fidelity to the Constitution

Article seven: describes the one time process of ratification of the document

Here is the text of the Constitution that was sent to the states for their ratifying conventions:

We the People *of the United States, in Order to form a more perfect Union, establish Justice, insure domestic Tranquility, provide for the common defence, promote the general Welfare, and secure the Blessings of Liberty to ourselves and our Posterity, do ordain and establish this Constitution for the United States of America.*

Article. I.

Section. 1.

All legislative Powers herein granted shall be vested in a Congress of the United States, which shall consist of a Senate and House of Representatives.

Section. 2.

The House of Representatives shall be composed of Members chosen every second Year by the People of the several States, and the Electors in each State shall have the Qualifications requisite for Electors of the most numerous Branch of the State Legislature.

No Person shall be a Representative who shall not have attained to the Age of twenty five Years, and been seven Years a Citizen of the United States, and who shall not, when elected, be an Inhabitant of that State in which he shall be chosen.

Representatives and direct Taxes shall be apportioned among the several States which may be included within this Union, according to their respective Numbers, which shall be determined by adding to the whole Number of free Persons, including those bound to Service for a Term of Years, and excluding Indians not taxed, three fifths of all other Persons. The actual Enumeration shall be made within three Years after the first Meeting of the Congress of the United States, and within every subsequent Term of ten Years, in such Manner as they shall by Law direct. The Number of Representatives shall not exceed one for every thirty Thousand, but each State shall have at Least one Representative; and until such enumeration shall be made, the State of New Hampshire shall be entitled to chuse three, Massachusetts eight, Rhode-Island and Providence Plantations one, Connecticut five, New-York six, New Jersey four, Pennsylvania eight, Delaware one, Maryland six, Virginia ten, North Carolina five, South Carolina five, and Georgia three.

When vacancies happen in the Representation from any State, the Executive Authority thereof shall issue Writs of Election to fill such Vacancies.

The House of Representatives shall chuse their Speaker and other Officers; and shall have the sole Power of Impeachment.

Section. 3.

The Senate of the United States shall be composed of two Senators from each State, chosen by the Legislature thereof, for six Years; and each Senator shall have one Vote.

Immediately after they shall be assembled in Consequence of the first Election, they shall be divided as equally as may be into three Classes. The Seats of the Senators of the first Class shall be vacated at the

Expiration of the second Year, of the second Class at the Expiration of the fourth Year, and of the third Class at the Expiration of the sixth Year, so that one third may be chosen every second Year; and if Vacancies happen by Resignation, or otherwise, during the Recess of the Legislature of any State, the Executive thereof may make temporary Appointments until the next Meeting of the Legislature, which shall then fill such Vacancies.

No Person shall be a Senator who shall not have attained to the Age of thirty Years, and been nine Years a Citizen of the United States, and who shall not, when elected, be an Inhabitant of that State for which he shall be chosen.

The Vice President of the United States shall be President of the Senate, but shall have no Vote, unless they be equally divided.

The Senate shall chuse their other Officers, and also a President pro tempore, in the Absence of the Vice President, or when he shall exercise the Office of President of the United States.

The Senate shall have the sole Power to try all Impeachments. When sitting for that Purpose, they shall be on Oath or Affirmation. When the President of the United States is tried, the Chief Justice shall preside: And no Person shall be convicted without the Concurrence of two thirds of the Members present.

Judgment in Cases of Impeachment shall not extend further than to removal from Office, and disqualification to hold and enjoy any Office of honor, Trust or Profit under the United States: but the Party convicted shall nevertheless be liable and subject to Indictment, Trial, Judgment and Punishment, according to Law.

Section. 4.

The Times, Places and Manner of holding Elections for Senators and Representatives, shall be prescribed in each State by the Legislature thereof; but the Congress may at any time by Law make or alter such Regulations, except as to the Places of chusing Senators.

The Congress shall assemble at least once in every Year, and such Meeting shall be on the first Monday in December, unless they shall by Law appoint a different Day.

Section. 5.

Each House shall be the Judge of the Elections, Returns and Qualifications of its own Members, and a Majority of each shall constitute a Quorum to do Business; but a smaller Number may adjourn from day to day, and may be authorized to compel the Attendance of absent Members, in such Manner, and under such Penalties as each House may provide.

Each House may determine the Rules of its Proceedings, punish its Members for disorderly Behaviour, and, with the Concurrence of two thirds, expel a Member.

Each House shall keep a Journal of its Proceedings, and from time to time publish the same, excepting such Parts as may in their Judgment require Secrecy; and the Yeas and Nays of the Members of either House on any question shall, at the Desire of one fifth of those Present, be entered on the Journal.

Neither House, during the Session of Congress, shall, without the Consent of the other, adjourn for more than three days, nor to any other Place than that in which the two Houses shall be sitting.

Section. 6.

The Senators and Representatives shall receive a Compensation for their Services, to be ascertained by Law, and paid out of the Treasury of the United States. They shall in all Cases, except Treason, Felony and Breach of the Peace, be privileged from Arrest during their Attendance at the Session of their respective Houses, and in going to and returning from the same; and for any Speech or Debate in either House, they shall not be questioned in any other Place.

No Senator or Representative shall, during the Time for which he was elected, be appointed to any civil Office under the Authority of the United States, which shall have been created, or the Emoluments whereof shall have been encreased during such time; and no Person holding any Office under the United States, shall be a Member of either House during his Continuance in Office.

Section. 7.

All Bills for raising Revenue shall originate in the House of Representatives; but the Senate may propose or concur with Amendments as on other Bills.

Every Bill which shall have passed the House of Representatives and the Senate, shall, before it become a Law, be presented to the President of the United States; If he approve he shall sign it, but if not he shall return it, with his Objections to that House in which it shall have originated, who shall enter the Objections at large on their Journal, and proceed to reconsider it. *If after such Reconsideration two thirds of that House shall agree to pass the Bill, it shall be sent, together with the Objections, to the other House, by which it shall likewise be reconsidered, and if approved by two thirds of that House, it shall become a Law. But in all such Cases the Votes of both Houses shall be determined by yeas and Nays, and the Names of the Persons voting for and against the Bill shall be entered on the Journal of each House respectively. If any Bill shall not be returned by the President within ten Days (Sundays excepted) after it shall have been presented to him, the Same shall be a Law, in like Manner as if he had signed it, unless the Congress by their Adjournment prevent its Return, in which Case it shall not be a Law.*

Every Order, Resolution, or Vote to which the Concurrence of the Senate and House of Representatives may be necessary (except on a question of Adjournment) shall be presented to the President of the United States; and before the Same shall take Effect, shall be approved by him, or being disapproved by him, shall be repassed by two thirds of the Senate and House of Representatives, according to the Rules and Limitations prescribed in the Case of a Bill.

Section. 8.

The Congress shall have Power To lay and collect Taxes, Duties, Imposts and Excises, to pay the Debts and provide for the common Defence and general Welfare of the United States; but all Duties, Imposts and Excises shall be uniform throughout the United States;

To borrow Money on the credit of the United States;

To regulate Commerce with foreign Nations, and among the several States, and with the Indian Tribes;

To establish an uniform Rule of Naturalization, and uniform Laws on the subject of Bankruptcies throughout the United States;

To coin Money, regulate the Value thereof, and of foreign Coin, and fix the Standard of Weights and Measures;

To provide for the Punishment of counterfeiting the Securities and current Coin of the United States;

To establish Post Offices and post Roads;

To promote the Progress of Science and useful Arts, by securing for limited Times to Authors and Inventors the exclusive Right to their respective Writings and Discoveries;

To constitute Tribunals inferior to the supreme Court;

To define and punish Piracies and Felonies committed on the high Seas, and Offences against the Law of Nations;

To declare War, grant Letters of Marque and Reprisal, and make Rules concerning Captures on Land and Water;

To raise and support Armies, but no Appropriation of Money to that Use shall be for a longer Term than two Years;

To provide and maintain a Navy;

To make Rules for the Government and Regulation of the land and naval Forces;

To provide for calling forth the Militia to execute the Laws of the Union, suppress Insurrections and repel Invasions;

To provide for organizing, arming, and disciplining, the Militia, and for governing such Part of them as may be employed in the Service of the United States, reserving to the States respectively, the Appointment of the Officers, and the Authority of training the Militia according to the discipline prescribed by Congress;

To exercise exclusive Legislation in all Cases whatsoever, over such District (not exceeding ten Miles square) as may, by Cession of particular States, and the Acceptance of Congress, become the Seat of the Government of the United States, and to exercise like Authority over all Places purchased by the Consent of the Legislature of the State in which the Same shall be, for the Erection of Forts, Magazines, Arsenals, dock-Yards, and other needful Buildings;—And

To make all Laws which shall be necessary and proper for carrying into Execution the foregoing Powers, and all other Powers vested by this Constitution in the Government of the United States, or in any Department or Officer thereof.

Section. 9.

The Migration or Importation of such Persons as any of the States now existing shall think proper to admit, shall not be prohibited by the Congress prior to the Year one thousand eight hundred and eight, but a Tax or duty may be imposed on such Importation, not exceeding ten dollars for each Person.

The Privilege of the Writ of Habeas Corpus shall not be suspended, unless when in Cases of Rebellion or Invasion the public Safety may require it.

No Bill of Attainder or ex post facto Law shall be passed.

No Capitation, or other direct, Tax shall be laid, unless in Proportion to the Census or enumeration herein before directed to be taken.

No Tax or Duty shall be laid on Articles exported from any State.

No Preference shall be given by any Regulation of Commerce or Revenue to the Ports of one State over those of another: nor shall Vessels bound to, or from, one State, be obliged to enter, clear, or pay Duties in another.

No Money shall be drawn from the Treasury, but in Consequence of Appropriations made by Law; and a regular Statement and Account of the Receipts and Expenditures of all public Money shall be published from time to time.

No Title of Nobility shall be granted by the United States: And no Person holding any Office of Profit or Trust under them, shall, without the Consent of the Congress, accept of any present, Emolument, Office, or Title, of any kind whatever, from any King, Prince, or foreign State.

Section. 10.

No State shall enter into any Treaty, Alliance, or Confederation; grant Letters of Marque and Reprisal; coin Money; emit Bills of Credit; make any Thing but gold and silver Coin a Tender in Payment of

Debts; pass any Bill of Attainder, ex post facto Law, or Law impairing the Obligation of Contracts, or grant any Title of Nobility.

No State shall, without the Consent of the Congress, lay any Imposts or Duties on Imports or Exports, except what may be absolutely necessary for executing it's inspection Laws: and the net Produce of all Duties and Imposts, laid by any State on Imports or Exports, shall be for the Use of the Treasury of the United States; and all such Laws shall be subject to the Revision and Controul of the Congress.

No State shall, without the Consent of Congress, lay any Duty of Tonnage, keep Troops, or Ships of War in time of Peace, enter into any Agreement or Compact with another State, or with a foreign Power, or engage in War, unless actually invaded, or in such imminent Danger as will not admit of delay.

Article. II.

Section. 1.

The executive Power shall be vested in a President of the United States of America. He shall hold his Office during the Term of four Years, and, together with the Vice President, chosen for the same Term, be elected, as follows

Each State shall appoint, in such Manner as the Legislature thereof may direct, a Number of Electors, equal to the whole Number of Senators and Representatives to which the State may be entitled in the Congress: but no Senator or Representative, or Person holding an Office of Trust or Profit under the United States, shall be appointed an Elector.

The Electors shall meet in their respective States, and vote by Ballot for two Persons, of whom one at least shall not be an Inhabitant of the same State with themselves. And they shall make a List of all the Persons voted for, and of the Number of Votes for each; which List they shall sign and certify, and transmit sealed to the Seat of the Government of the United States, directed to the President of the Senate. The President of the Senate shall, in the Presence of the Senate and House of Representatives, open all the Certificates, and the Votes shall then be counted. The Person having the greatest Number of Votes shall be the President, if such Number be a Majority of the whole Number of Electors appointed; and if there be more than one who have such Majority, and have an equal Number of Votes, then the House of Representatives shall immediately chuse by Ballot one of them for President; and if no Person have a Majority, then from the five highest on the List the said House shall in like Manner chuse the President. But in chusing the President, the Votes shall be taken by States, the Representation from each State having one Vote; A quorum for this Purpose shall consist of a Member or Members from two thirds of the States, and a Majority of all the States shall be necessary to a Choice. In every Case, after the Choice of the President, the Person having the greatest Number of Votes of the Electors shall be the Vice President. But if there should remain two or more who have equal Votes, the Senate shall chuse from them by Ballot the Vice President.

The Congress may determine the Time of chusing the Electors, and the Day on which they shall give their Votes; which Day shall be the same throughout the United States.

No Person except a natural born Citizen, or a Citizen of the United States, at the time of the Adoption of this Constitution, shall be eligible to the Office of President; neither shall any Person be eligible to that

Office who shall not have attained to the Age of thirty five Years, and been fourteen Years a Resident within the United States.

In Case of the Removal of the President from Office, or of his Death, Resignation, or Inability to discharge the Powers and Duties of the said Office, the Same shall devolve on the Vice President, and the Congress may by Law provide for the Case of Removal, Death, Resignation or Inability, both of the President and Vice President, declaring what Officer shall then act as President, and such Officer shall act accordingly, until the Disability be removed, or a President shall be elected.

The President shall, at stated Times, receive for his Services, a Compensation, which shall neither be encreased nor diminished during the Period for which he shall have been elected, and he shall not receive within that Period any other Emolument from the United States, or any of them.

Before he enter on the Execution of his Office, he shall take the following Oath or Affirmation:—"I do solemnly swear (or affirm) that I will faithfully execute the Office of President of the United States, and will to the best of my Ability, preserve, protect and defend the Constitution of the United States."

Section. 2.

The President shall be Commander in Chief of the Army and Navy of the United States, and of the Militia of the several States, when called into the actual Service of the United States; he may require the Opinion, in writing, of the principal Officer in each of the executive Departments, upon any Subject relating to the Duties of their respective Offices, and he shall have Power to grant Reprieves and Pardons for Offences against the United States, except in Cases of Impeachment.

He shall have Power, by and with the Advice and Consent of the Senate, to make Treaties, provided two thirds of the Senators present concur; and he shall nominate, and by and with the Advice and Consent of the Senate, shall appoint Ambassadors, other public Ministers and Consuls, Judges of the supreme Court, and all other Officers of the United States, whose Appointments are not herein otherwise provided for, and which shall be established by Law: but the Congress may by Law vest the Appointment of such inferior Officers, as they think proper, in the President alone, in the Courts of Law, or in the Heads of Departments.

The President shall have Power to fill up all Vacancies that may happen during the Recess of the Senate, by granting Commissions which shall expire at the End of their next Session.

Section. 3.

He shall from time to time give to the Congress Information of the State of the Union, and recommend to their Consideration such Measures as he shall judge necessary and expedient; he may, on extraordinary Occasions, convene both Houses, or either of them, and in Case of Disagreement between them, with Respect to the Time of Adjournment, he may adjourn them to such Time as he shall think proper; he shall receive Ambassadors and other public Ministers; he shall take Care that the Laws be faithfully executed, and shall Commission all the Officers of the United States.

Section. 4.

The President, Vice President and all civil Officers of the United States, shall be removed from Office on Impeachment for, and Conviction of, Treason, Bribery, or other high Crimes and Misdemeanors.

Article III.

Section. 1.

The judicial Power of the United States, shall be vested in one supreme Court, and in such inferior Courts as the Congress may from time to time ordain and establish. The Judges, both of the supreme and inferior Courts, shall hold their Offices during good Behaviour, and shall, at stated Times, receive for their Services, a Compensation, which shall not be diminished during their Continuance in Office.

Section. 2.

The judicial Power shall extend to all Cases, in Law and Equity, arising under this Constitution, the Laws of the United States, and Treaties made, or which shall be made, under their Authority;—to all Cases affecting Ambassadors, other public Ministers and Consuls;—to all Cases of admiralty and maritime Jurisdiction;—to Controversies to which the United States shall be a Party;—to Controversies between two or more States;— between a State and Citizens of another State,— between Citizens of different States,—between Citizens of the same State claiming Lands under Grants of different States, and between a State, or the Citizens thereof, and foreign States, Citizens or Subjects.

In all Cases affecting Ambassadors, other public Ministers and Consuls, and those in which a State shall be Party, the supreme Court shall have original Jurisdiction. In all the other Cases before mentioned, the supreme Court shall have appellate Jurisdiction, both as to Law and Fact, with such Exceptions, and under such Regulations as the Congress shall make.

The Trial of all Crimes, except in Cases of Impeachment, shall be by Jury; and such Trial shall be held in the State where the said Crimes shall have been committed; but when not committed within any State, the Trial shall be at such Place or Places as the Congress may by Law have directed.

Section. 3.

Treason against the United States, shall consist only in levying War against them, or in adhering to their Enemies, giving them Aid and Comfort. No Person shall be convicted of Treason unless on the Testimony of two Witnesses to the same overt Act, or on Confession in open Court.

The Congress shall have Power to declare the Punishment of Treason, but no Attainder of Treason shall work Corruption of Blood, or Forfeiture except during the Life of the Person attainted.

Article. IV.

Section. 1.

Full Faith and Credit shall be given in each State to the public Acts, Records, and judicial Proceedings of every other State. And the Congress may by general Laws prescribe the Manner in which such Acts, Records and Proceedings shall be proved, and the Effect thereof.

Section. 2.

The Citizens of each State shall be entitled to all Privileges and Immunities of Citizens in the several States.
A Person charged in any State with Treason, Felony, or other Crime, who shall flee from Justice, and be found in another State, shall on Demand of the executive Authority of the State from which he fled, be delivered up, to be removed to the State having Jurisdiction of the Crime.

No Person held to Service or Labour in one State, under the Laws thereof, escaping into another, shall, in Consequence of any Law or Regulation therein, be discharged from such Service or Labour, but shall be delivered up on Claim of the Party to whom such Service or Labour may be due.

Section. 3.

New States may be admitted by the Congress into this Union; but no new State shall be formed or erected within the Jurisdiction of any other State; nor any State be formed by the Junction of two or more States, or Parts of States, without the Consent of the Legislatures of the States concerned as well as of the Congress.

The Congress shall have Power to dispose of and make all needful Rules and Regulations respecting the Territory or other Property belonging to the United States; and nothing in this Constitution shall be so construed as to Prejudice any Claims of the United States, or of any particular State.

Section. 4.

The United States shall guarantee to every State in this Union a Republican Form of Government, and shall protect each of them against Invasion; and on Application of the Legislature, or of the Executive (when the Legislature cannot be convened), against domestic Violence.

Article. V.

The Congress, whenever two thirds of both Houses shall deem it necessary, shall propose Amendments to this Constitution, or, on the Application of the Legislatures of two thirds of the several States, shall call a Convention for proposing Amendments, which, in either Case, shall be valid to all Intents and Purposes, as Part of this Constitution, when ratified by the Legislatures of three fourths of the several States, or by Conventions in three fourths thereof, as the one or the other Mode of Ratification may be proposed by the Congress; Provided that no Amendment which may be made prior to the Year One thousand eight hundred and eight shall in any Manner affect the first and fourth Clauses in the Ninth Section of the first Article; and that no State, without its Consent, shall be deprived of its equal Suffrage in the Senate.

Article. VI.

All Debts contracted and Engagements entered into, before the Adoption of this Constitution, shall be as valid against the United States under this Constitution, as under the Confederation.

This Constitution, and the Laws of the United States which shall be made in Pursuance thereof; and all Treaties made, or which shall be made, under the Authority of the United States, shall be the supreme Law of the Land; and the Judges in every State shall be bound thereby, any Thing in the Constitution or Laws of any State to the Contrary notwithstanding.

The Senators and Representatives before mentioned, and the Members of the several State Legislatures, and all executive and judicial Officers, both of the United States and of the several States, shall be bound by Oath or Affirmation, to support this Constitution; but no religious Test shall ever be required as a Qualification to any Office or public Trust under the United States.

Article. VII.

The Ratification of the Conventions of nine States, shall be sufficient for the Establishment of this Constitution between the States so ratifying the Same.

The Word, "the," being interlined between the seventh and eighth Lines of the first Page, The Word "Thirty" being partly written on an Erazure in the fifteenth Line of the first Page, The Words "is tried" being interlined between the thirty second and thirty third Lines of the first Page and the Word "the" being interlined between the forty third and forty fourth Lines of the second Page.

Attest William Jackson Secretary done in Convention by the Unanimous Consent of the States present the Seventeenth Day of September in the Year of our Lord one thousand seven hundred and Eighty seven and of the Independance of the United States of America the Twelfth In witness whereof We have hereunto subscribed our Names,

G.Washington
President and deputy from Virginia[2]

CHAPTER 4.

GAINING CONSENT FOR A MORE PERFECT UNION

~~~~~~~~~~~~~~~~~~~~~~~~~

That's it. That is the entire Constitution of the United States as forwarded to the states for ratification.

Within a week or so of September 17, 1787, when the Constitution was unanimously voted on in Philadelphia at the Constitutional Convention, and then submitted to the states for ratification, anti-Constitutional forces began publishing a series of essays articulating their opposition to the new form of government. Article Seven of the Constitution required at least nine of the states to ratify the document for it to go into effect, but it was desired that all thirteen states ratify it so as to not have states brought into the union against their will. So again, we see the states giving birth to the nation, not some heretofore unknown central government usurping states authority. At the center of this approach is one of the Declaration of Independence's foundational tenets; that legitimate government can only be derived from the *Consent of the governed*. The concerns of the founders regarding the totalitarian rule, either from a King or a legislature was universal. Today people who bring up the Constitution and its government limiting powers are too often considered "right-wing nuts" or "extremists" however during the ratification process between 1787 and into 1789 and beyond it was not the pro-Constitutional federalists who were seeking the most limits on government, it was the anti-Constitution anti-federalists who sought the smallest and most limited central government. Our country was founded by two groups of people, those who distrusted the government and those who really distrusted the government.

A full-on public relations campaign ensued shortly thereafter when three strongly pro-Constitutional federalists joined together to publish a series of essays in response to the anti-federalists, (who were on their own, albeit less coordinated, campaign) and in support of the Constitution and the new form of government. Alexander Hamilton and John Jay from New York and James Madison from Virginia, under the joint pseudonym *Publius,* began publishing essays in several New York newspapers to garner the support of that large, central and essential state. In all, the goal of the eighty-five essays, collectively known as The Federalist, penned by Publius was to articulate to the people in the states exactly what was in the new Constitution, why a stronger central government was necessary, how the structure of the new government's system of checks and balances protected states and individual rights and to generally defend the document and the new form of government while publishing so frequently that it would be difficult for the opposition to mount an effective response.

The major themes that Publius discussed in the Federalist included the general necessity for a strong union to limit foreign force and influence, to ameliorate potential dissensions between and among the states, to coordinate foreign trade on the continent, to institute a Navy, to gain economies of a single governmental organization (as opposed to each state needing to fulfill those limited roles that are logically centralized), Publius addressed some of the defects of the Article of Confederation in their argument for the new government, and they discussed taxation powers, republicanism, checks, and balances and the structure and roles of the three proposed branches of the new government.

The coordinated strategy of Publius was met with a much less coordinated, but nonetheless vigorous campaign by the Anti-Federalists. Published under names like Cato, the Federal Farmer and Brutus the Anti-Federalists were also patriots and founding fathers. Patrick Henry, Richard Henry Lee and George Mason of Virginia, James Winthrop and Samuel Adams of Massachusetts and George Clinton and Melancton Smith of New York fought a pitched battle with Publius in the press and in speeches. The Anti-Federalist's efforts continued even past the ratification of the Constitution. A note of interest, as theirs was not as coordinated an effort, as was that of Publius, the Anti-Federalists did not match the eighty-five essays of the Federalist's *tit for tat* as is often believed, the communications of the Anti-Federalists were broader and included, not only newspapers but pamphlets and speeches as well. The anonymous naming using monikers from classical antiquity like Publius, Cato, and Brutus was commonplace at the time and was used for a variety of reasons including the simple desire to be anonymous when voicing unpopular positions against, for example, a monarch. The naming also could give the appearance of a single voice in the case of Publius where there were multiple authors, and as many of the founders were steeped in classical studies the particular name chosen by the author could take on some import as they attempted to align themselves with classical figures who possessed certain moral or other attributes.

The ratification process was hitting substantial headwinds from several of the states. Virginia, New York, and Massachusetts were among the most vocal about their distrust of the proposed new government. The state's distrust was generally around centralizing too much power, as the states were enjoying their newfound freedom from the crown and didn't want to relinquish control to another potential tyrant. The single most significant resistance to the new Constitution was that it lacked the concept of an individual Bill of Rights.

The subject of a Bill of Rights had come up at the convention but was not advanced because the delegates were primarily focused on the structure of the new government, and they believed that the document's primary feature of separation of powers and the checks and balances and the specific delineation of centralized powers would ensure that individual and states' rights would be adequately protected. In hindsight, the Constitution's substantial increase in centralized power as compared to the Articles of Confederation made the states ill at ease enough that it became clear that a Bill of Rights would be required for the Constitution to be ratified.

Among the states where ratification faced a significant challenge was Massachusetts. However, two influential anti-federalists and patriots John Hancock and Samuel Adams proposed what came to be known as the Massachusetts Compromise, whereby the anti-federalists would support ratification provided that should the Constitution be adopted there would be amendments considered, including a Bill of Rights. The federalists agreed to the compromise and Massachusetts voted to ratify. Several other states adopted this same approach and by September of 1788 the Continental Congress voted to put the Constitution into effect with the 11 states that had ratified the document (North Carolina and Rhode Island were the last two states, ratifying in November 1789 and May 1790 respectively) effective March 4, 1789. George Washington would be inaugurated as the first President of the United States two months later on April 30, 1789. Our new Constitution and the government that it created was now in place.

In accordance with the agreement struck with the anti-federalists, the first Congress under the new Constitution took up several amendments. During the first Congress there were twelve amendments put forward, and ten amendments were passed. Those amendments became known as the Bill of Rights.

So, let's stop for a moment and see where we are. The colonies became fed up with being ill-treated subjects of the English crown, they take an incredible stance, influenced by *the Enlightenment*, stating that they have the inalienable right to equal standing with the crown, they fight a war with the most powerful empire in the world under a loose confederation of the colonies. After defeating the British, they begin to recognize the weakness of their confederation, act to improve upon it and bring all of the states along to create a new Constitutional republic and pass the first ten amendments to the Constitution, the Bill of Rights, all over the course of just 16 years. Impressive.

Let's look at the government that the founders put in place. I am not going to go through each and every section and clause; instead, I will highlight those parts that clearly evidence the direct path from the Declaration of Independence's ideas to this new form of government. I will pay special attention to do three things. First will be, where applicable, to show the founders' desire for a limited government and that that government shall be instituted with the *consent of the governed*. Second I will highlight those places that point back to the Declaration of Independence's idea that *all men are created equal*. And third, I will point out the areas that make it evident that the originalist view of the Constitution is the only intellectually honest way to understand the document. As a note, I think it is necessary to clarify, until this point, primarily in the discussion of the ratification process, I have used the term "anti-Constitution" to describe the anti-federalists. The anti-federalists were only anti-Constitution because they did not think that the Constitution did enough to limit the power of the central government. From this point on, when I use the term anti-Constitution, I am referring to another creature altogether. I am referring to those individuals who seek to misinterpret, ignore or nullify the document purposefully.

Let's start with the Constitution's preamble.

We the People of the United States, in Order to form a more perfect Union, establish Justice, insure domestic Tranquility, provide for the common defense, promote the general Welfare, and secure the Blessings of Liberty to ourselves and our Posterity, do ordain and establish this Constitution for the United States of America[1].

The preamble intends to set a general context for what follows in the Constitution's various articles. The phrase *a more perfect union* is a simple recognition of the necessity to form a government more effective than the government under the Articles of Confederation. The words chosen by the drafters are again critical as we will continue to see throughout the document. The preamble moves to the phrase *provide for the common defense* the word provide is used because the defense of the nation is a role for the central government. The word *'provide'* contrasts to the word *promote,* as in the next phrase, *promote the general Welfare.* The word promote means that the central government will advocate for the general welfare. The word *general* is a direct link to the Declaration of Independence's *all men are created equal*, as the founders put a government in place for *all*, for everyone, the general public, not a government designed to balkanize for the benefit of special interests into which today's policies have devolved. Additionally, the term *general welfare* is a phrase too often abused today by those with anti-Constitutional goals seeking to have it reference wealth transfer programs. The operative word in the phrase *general welfare* is *general*, not *welfare*.

As we move into the various articles contained within the body of the Constitution, we have a clear link to the Declaration of Independence's *consent of the governed*.

The delegates at the Constitutional Convention submitted the Constitution to the states to consider for ratification. The delegates clearly, obviously and naturally realized they required *consent* from the states. Keep in mind that at the time of the Constitutional convention the country was still operating under the Articles of Confederation, which required unanimous consent from the states to do anything whatsoever.

So, within the Constitution's text, the convention's delegates discreetly articulated the functions for which they were requesting purview over and submitted that text to the states. (Incidentally, stylistically the process of specific delineation is consistent with the Declaration of Independence in that grievances suffered under the crown were thoroughly and explicitly articulated as well).

A strong argument for an originalist view of the Constitution emerges around one of our central themes, *the consent of the governed*.

We have established that the states needed to consent to relinquish certain specific, finite, and limited governmental functions. We have also established that the states were sufficiently reticent about a strong central government that they required an agreement to include certain rights protecting amendments (the Bill of Rights) to be brought up in the first Congress for the states to agree to ratify the document.

The states required clarity regarding the specific powers to be granted to the central government, particular protection of state's and citizens' rights (through proposing a Bill of Rights) and a specific role for the states in the structure of the central government through both the method of electing the executive, the composition of the senate and the through the amendment process. The states needed to specifically continue to consent to their being governed through the entire process.

Why then after the republic is established under these clear, specific and agreed to terms, under this requirement for the governed to consent, would the states no longer need to be asked when more power is to be stripped away and centralized? They would not, and they did not.

What then is the intellectually honest countervailing argument justifying the massive federal usurpation of states and individual rights? Through activist courts, a tyrannical legislative branch and an even more out of control bureaucracy neither the states nor their citizens are asked if they agree to be tormented but tormented we are.

Ironically, it is actually the brevity, simplicity, clarity and limiting nature of the Constitution and that it can only change in concrete ways that compel the anti-Constitutionalists to attempt to tell the public that the Constitution is complex, indecipherable, outdated, written by rich white, slaveholders or that it is a "living and breathing" document. The anti-Constitutionalists knows the explicit nature of the Constitution; they just don't want you to understand the nature of the Constitution as it will thwart their illegitimate political goals. This is why I say that an originalist view is the only intellectually honest view. The anti-Constitutionalist does not like the limits the Constitution contains; they don't want to have to ask for your consent to rule over you. So they lie. An exclamation point is put on this issue when we get to the Bill of Rights' 10th amendment.

Think of the two different ways in which the Constitution can be interpreted (only one of which is legitimate), either originalist or 'living and breathing.' In the originalist view, while there is certainly some debate around the exact original meaning of individual sections, it is around smallish issues and not around the broad themes, the debates are contained. Among originalists, there is no debate around the general nature of the Constitution, that the central government is limited to those consented to powers.

For the anti-constitutionalist and his notions of a living and breathing Constitution, the entire document can be thrown out the window. Under this notion, the Constitution has, literally, an infinite number of meanings. Depending on the reader, the day of the week, the time of day, the Constitution's meaning somehow magically morphs. In the process of continually changing the Constitution's meaning the notion of consent of the governed also is necessarily dismissed; we agreed to the original meaning, we were never asked to consent to the new meaning. Another victim of the living and breathing argument is the separation of powers. If the final arbiter of Constitutional meaning is the Supreme Court and justices have a living and breathing view of the Constitution aren't then Justices making law and not adjudicating it?

Let's get into the text of the document we'll start by looking at the first of the Constitution's seven articles. First I'll describe the structure of each Article, then we'll get into several of the sections in more detail, again with the goal of highlighting places that point back to the Declaration of Independence's concepts of *consent of the governed* and *all men are created equal* as well as drawing attention to instances that make the argument for an originalist view of the Constitution.

CHAPTER 5:

ARTICLE ONE, THE LEGISLATIVE BRANCH

A rticle One simply describes the make-up of, qualifications for, and role of the legislative branch of the central government. Article One has ten sections. I process the structure of Article One like this:

Section One describes the overarching purpose of the legislative branch

Sections Two through Six establish the two houses of Congress (the House of Representatives and the Senate). It establishes the qualifications necessary to be elected to each house, the manner by which representatives and senators are elected, their respective terms of office, how often they must convene and how they are to be paid. .

Section Seven describes the legislative process, how bills become laws

Section Eight describes what Congress can do

Section Nine describes what Congress can't do

Section Ten Describes what the States can't do

This seems pretty simple and straight-forward, we must get to the in-decipherable part later. Article One certainly is understandable and plainly and logically constructed. I hope the reader is getting irritated that there are those among us that don't think you can process and understand the Constitution. Now we'll look at some of the sections, Article One, Section One is one of my favorites (I must admit I have lots of favorites). It says, in total:

All legislative Powers herein granted shall be vested in a Congress of the United States, which shall consist of a Senate and House of Representatives.[1]

That's it, twenty-five words describing what Congress' role is. And it is powerful when looked at in context with the Declaration of Independence. Remember this grievance from the list that was in the Declaration of Independence?

He has erected a multitude of New Offices, and sent hither swarms of Officers to harrass our people, and eat out their substance.[2]

I think of this grievance from the Declaration as the "we hate bureaucrats" grievance. A bureaucrat is at best an un-elected, un-accountable necessity for instituting laws, duly passed, by those who *are* accountable, those who need consent from the governed. The founders knew from their experience that a bureaucrat run amok is another thing altogether. So Congress has a simple answer. The very first thing that the Constitution says after the preamble is that *all* laws that the central government has jurisdiction over come out of Congress, period. So why then today do we have score upon score of departments and agencies and their army of unelected, unaccountable bureaucrats making laws? The bureaucrats call them rules or regulations, or whatever, but when I can get fined or go to jail, it's a law. There is no possible way to consent to a bureaucrat, you have no relationship with him, and he has no standing in your life, yet he illegally seizes power, torments you and the President, Congress and the courts let him. What of separation of powers? Was not the concept of separation of powers essential to the states ceding power to the central government during the ratification? If a bureaucrat can make laws, how is that separation? Let me see if I understand this correctly. The anti-constitutionalist advocates for all three branches of the central government making laws? Apparently so. We have seen that Congress has the authority to make laws and through the notion of a 'living and breathing' Constitution the judiciary can make laws, and through an out of control bureaucracy the Executive branch can make laws, what of this have you consented to? As we have seen, the entire birth of the Constitution was based on *the consent of the governed* so by Congress saying the concise words of Article One, Section One they are saying to the people that through our representative republic the people will have the final say over what the government can do to them.

Far from complex, the constitution is simple, understandable traceable to our Declaration of Independence, Article One, Section One also speaks to the necessarily limited nature of the federal government as Congress is the only legislating body for those issues over which they have jurisdiction. There is no provision whatsoever for Congress to delegate Article One, Section One powers (or any other powers for that matter). The delegates to the Constitutional Convention also put in a requirement that Congress must meet at least once a year, so they clearly were not envisioning an overbearing and burdensome administrative state. Somehow the anti-Constitutionalist refuses to understand the plain language of Article One,

Section One, mostly they just don't want you to understand it because then they could never do things to you for which you did not consent.

Sections Two through Six establish and apportion Congress' two houses. I think there are a couple of particularly essential items in these sections. First, what the sections are saying is again wholly consistent with the principles we've discussed contained in the Declaration of Independence. By having elected officials making laws there inherently exists at least some accountability, through the election process that should advance the concept of *consent of the governed*. I view the qualifications and terms of office as an administrative necessity. Clearly, the states give birth to our federal government; evidenced by the numerical equality of senators from each state (two) and the means by which they are elected; by state legislatures. Continually and consistently, we see that there was no intent by the states to cede plenary power to a centralized government.

We see further erosion of the Constitution's original intent with the recent Supreme Court Ruling on whether or not a question of Citizenship can be included in the Census. Congress gets the requirement to perform a census in Article One, Section Two of the Constitution, it says:

The actual Enumeration shall be made within three Years after the first Meeting of the Congress of the United States, and within every subsequent Term of ten Years, in such Manner as they shall by Law direct[3]

The section within which the requirement is included is explicitly trying to apportion representation in Congress. The way you get to Congress is to be voted in. Who votes? Citizens. Therefore perhaps the only question the census should be asking is how many citizens live here. The census has been turned into some form of social justice survey to which I have not consented. How is it that we can ask virtually every question pertaining to race and sex on the long-form census but not ask about citizenship? Once again, the argument is somehow moved from fact-based and logical to emotional, and our founding document is further bastardized.

Article One, Section Seven of the Constitution describes how federal laws are made. From my perspective, two items of particular note are contained in the section. First, the opening sentence says:

All Bills for raising Revenue shall originate in the House of Representatives; but the Senate may propose or concur with Amendments as on other Bills.[4]

I view this sentence similarly to the opening sentence of Article One, Section One where it is made clear that *all* laws come out of Congress. Here it is saying very plainly (I don't need a time machine to understand) that all bills about raising federal revenue originate in Congress' House of Representatives. That's *all* federal revenue. So the unelected bureaucracy can't tax you, only those who you have, by their election, consented to can. So how legitimate are the fees, surcharges, etc. that the administrative state burdens us with? Surely fees, surcharges, etc. would fall under *All*, wouldn't they?

The other noteworthy (extremely) Item in Article One, Section Seven is the manifestation of our federal government's system of checks and balances. Congress has the responsibility for crafting legislation for issues over which the central government has jurisdiction, a bill needs to pass both houses of Congress, and then that bill needs to get executive approval, or if denied that support, the bill can still become law by a two-thirds vote by each of the houses.

Simple and genius. Unfortunately, from my perspective, Article One Section Five gives each house the ability make its own rules around their own proceedings and that has, over time, resulting in some arcane parliamentary procedures that complicate a process that needn't be complicated.

Now we move onto, what I think of as, "the big one," Article One Section Eight. Article One Section Eight of the Constitution delineates what it is that Congress can do. And if, as we have learned, all laws come out of Congress Article One Section Eight is really defining virtually every single thing that the federal government has purview over. So it must be huge, right? Nope. Complex, right? Nope. I count only about 26 discreet items (you may count slightly more or less), but that is it. Let's take a look at some of the highlights of what the federal government has purview over and again link it to the Declaration of Independence and see where we can find a nod to the case for Constitutional originalism.

We'll start with perhaps the most abused of the limitations placed on the federal government; the infamous commerce clause. It states the Congress has authority:

To regulate Commerce with foreign Nations, and among the several States, and with the Indian Tribes[5]

So much wrong has been done to this simple clause that I hardly know where to begin. Let's start with the clear and simple origins of the clause. Remember the intention of the Annapolis Convention? The Annapolis Convention attempted to resolve trade issues that had emerged due to the weaknesses of the Articles of Confederation. States had begun taxing one another and were beginning to establish relations (trade and otherwise) with foreign Nations. In the first several Federalist papers that made the arguments for the need for Union, these were key issues. So, *in order to form a more perfect Union,* i.e., remedy some of the shortcomings of the Articles of Confederation, the central government should take over these logically centralized tasks. O.K. I'm fine with that. This clause being in the Constitution means the delegates to the convention asked the states to consent to these powers being centralized. We will continue to see that words matter. There is a reason that the word *'with'* is used, as in *To regulate Commerce 'with' foreign Nations.* It was the central government that would be negotiating directly *with* the foreign entities on behalf of the States. Pretty straightforward, right? The next phrase is *and among the several States.* Among. Not *'with',* because why would the central government need to regulate commerce *'with'* the states as the central government itself has nothing to trade. And certainly not *within.* The states would never (ever) give birth to a central government with plenary authority to regulate commerce *within* their state. Never. The word *among* is chosen because that is what this phrase in the Constitution is plainly attempting to remedy trade disputes between the states that arose from the weakness of the Articles of Confederation. The federal government would be granted the authority under the new Constitution to ensure the free flow of goods *among* the states. We know that trade issues among the states were a primary reason for the Annapolis Convention, which then led directly to the Constitutional convention being called in Philadelphia. So, if the obvious, clear, specific and traceable intent to which the states consented was only to regulate trade *among* the several states why then do I have a tag placed on my mattress by the federal government? Well, as all tyrants do, our government opened up an un-Constitutional loop hole that effectively said that commerce within a state affects commerce among the states and even choosing not to participate in commerce is participating in commerce. Really? But, the states consented to only *among the several states.*

Moreover, if the federal government's role was to actually ensure the free flow of trade among the states why is it that I cannot buy health insurance across state lines? The federal government encroaches where they have no authority and neglects their consented to role. So, instead of Congress simply regulating trade among the states and establishing those rules accordingly, we end up with scores of agencies and their unaccountable legions of bureaucrats tormenting every aspect of our lives. Those with mal-intent can rationalize anything, they'll tell you that 1+1=3 if that's what it takes to get their way. They'll tell you it's complicated and you couldn't understand it, then they show an inane formula like this:

a=b
ab=b2
ab−a2=b2−a2
a(b−a)=(b+a)(b−a)
a=b+a
a+1=b+a+1
a+1=2a+1
1+1=2+1
1+1=3

But you know that it's not complicated and 1+1=2 and among means among.

The fact that the commerce clause is being so, and increasingly, abused is strong evidence that our society's ignorance of the Constitution is the root cause of the abuse. When anti-constitutionalist politicians claim the commerce clause gives them the authority to regulate some part of our economy over which they have no purview, the uninformed citizen hears *commerce clause* and incorrectly assumes that the government must have standing. I would further argue that it is the rare politician that would know (much less care) that he is violating the fundamental relationship the government is allowed to have with our civil society.

Let's now look at what Article One Section Eight says about immigration, remember this grievance from the Declaration of Independence?

He has endeavoured to prevent the population of these States; for that purpose obstructing the Laws for Naturalization of Foreigners; refusing to pass others to encourage their migrations hither, and raising the conditions of new Appropriations of Lands.[6]

To thwart geographic and population growth in the colonies, the crown refused to institute laws and policies that would encourage and facilitate growth. The delegates at the convention asked the states to consent to have the new central government assume duties regarding establishing uniform rules regarding immigration. And of course, the rule would be uniform because the Constitution is implemented for the General Welfare. The language used to assume that authority was typically succinct. It says:

To establish an uniform Rule of Naturalization, and uniform Laws on the subject of Bankruptcies throughout the United States;[7]

So what then are sanctuary cities? The abuse of this clause is the opposite of what we typically see with the anti-Constitutionalist in the central government illegally assuming authority, here we see the anti-constitutionalists within the states (and cities) illegally inserting themselves into the responsibilities they ceded to the central government. The explicit, unambiguous language granting authority of immigration and naturalization is rarely discussed; instead, the anti-Constitutionalist will attempt to confuse the public with emotional arguments about breaking up families, and "dreamers," nonsense. As we discussed earlier, the Declaration of Independence's idea that *all men are created equal* means we are all equal under the law and that the Constitution is instituted for the *General Welfare* of the people, the citizenry. These two fundamental founding principles certainly do not align with the concept of certain people not having to obey the law. Why is it that just those people don't have to follow the law, why is it only those laws that don't have to be obeyed? Who are these people determining who does and who does not have to comply with the country's laws? I am confident that if I said, I live in a "tax sanctuary," the gentlemen from the Treasury Department would stop by my house with a nice orange suit for me to wear. The purposeful selective enforcement of laws places us just one step away from anarchy, the absence of law. America is supposed to be a nation of laws, not men. Laws that are just, laws that do not infringe on our God-given unalienable rights, laws to which we have consented. We citizens need to continually reaffirm our commitment to our founding principles to keep our republic from continuing to slip away.

A common misconception about the federal government is around the courts. Because the structure of the central government has three co-equal branches, legislative, executive, and judicial, many believe that it is the Supreme Court that establishes the other federal courts. It is not the Supreme Court, it is the Congress that establishes all inferior federal courts. Again with clear language in Article One, Section Eight:

To constitute Tribunals inferior to the Supreme Court;[8]

Yet Congress tolerates "liberal" courts. How can a court be liberal? As we are seeing the Constitution is really just not that difficult, and any interpretation by a judge other than an originalist view is legislating. And if *All Men are created equal* and we are all equal under the law, why should "judge shopping" exist. Judge shopping is a process whereby attorneys seek districts they believe will be sympathetic to their position on a particular issue. Shouldn't the accused expect the same result irrespective of the venue? With an originalist view of the Constitution, I believe that you would almost always expect the same outcome. With a "living, breathing" view of the Constitution we're back to 1+1=3, chaos and anarchy.

What other legal documents can you think of that has a meaning that changes over time? Can you imagine going to your bank and saying after ten years of paying on a thirty-year mortgage that you think that is enough, that you believe the intent of the mortgage contract could be interpreted to mean just pay for a while and that'll be good enough (even though it clearly says no such thing)? Or alternatively, after you are done paying off your mortgage the bank coming back to you and demanding another thirty years? Ludicrous. Or in today's sports dominated culture can you imagine Phil Mickelson (I'm a lefty too) picking up his ball six inches from the cup and saying, 'that was close enough' or Tom Brady taking a fifth down (notice how I didn't say underinflating footballs)? Of course, these examples are unimaginable and create unfair and unpredictable outcomes that are violative of the rules of those games so too is the notion of a liberal court, through its creative interpretations, making up law out of whole cloth in violation of the Constitution's separation of powers. Yet we see half a million Americans protest a football call and it is virtually crickets when it comes to our outrage over "bad calls" in Washington. Surely as a people, we must know the rules of our republic better than those of some game.

Unlike the insane examples above, the Constitution says what it says, in plain language and the only reason that the anti-constitutionalist judge, lawyer, politician or pundit advocates for something other than the logical originalist view is because they don't like that view and the process that the founders put in place to change the Constitution is too burdensome for them (as we'll see when we get to Article five) so instead they choose to nullify the Constitution. They all rely on an uninformed public to pull off this fraud. This reckless lawlessness masquerading as a legitimate argument is a, if not the primary source of erosion of our republic.

Article One, Section Eight, also grants the legislative branch of the central government authority to do other, logically centralized, functions including:

Congress can declare war, provide for a navy, raise armies, call forth the militia, and fight piracy. The central governments will coin money, deal with counterfeiting and bankruptcies, issue patents, set up a Post Office, and establish the seat of government. All of these are activities that make sense for a central government to control. So why are we so far afield from this original intent? A primary reason is again the power-hungry and deceitful anti-Constitutionalist. Let's look at the last clause of the Constitution's Article One, Section Eight. It says:

To make all Laws which shall be necessary and proper for carrying into Execution the foregoing Powers, and all other Powers vested by this Constitution in the Government of the United States, or in any Department or Officer thereof.[9]

This is the infamous *necessary and proper* clause.

This is what James Madison said on this issue:

"Nothing is more natural or common than first to use a general phrase, and then to explain or qualify it by a recital of particulars." Congress' ability to spend was to be confined by the more specific enumerated powers that immediately followed the "general welfare" clause.[10]

The Necessary and Proper clause makes one of the most robust cases that the anti-Constitutionalist is either purposefully violating the Constitution or has a reading disability or both. Often, when the anti-Constitutionalist legislator is pressed on why they feel they have authority that they do not have (which happens all too infrequently), they rely on this clause. They will say that they can do anything *necessary and proper.* This is why, if I feel like giving the anti-Constitutionalist a break, I say they may just have a reading disability. They stop reading the clause in mid-sentence, prior to the operative phrase. The central government does not have the power to do anything it feels is *necessary and proper.* The delegates at the Constitution convention asked the states for the legislative branch of the central government to be granted purview over 26 (more or less) discreet and delineated functions. By ratifying the Constitution, the states said O.K. *They consented.* So why, after painstakingly articulating specific powers, asking for and receiving permission to be granted those powers by the states, would the delegates end the section by saying 'and anything else we want to do.' They would not, and they did not. What they did say is typically clear and unambiguous, they said *necessary and proper for carrying into execution the foregoing powers.* Meaning 'we can make laws related to all the stuff we just listed.' That's it, only laws related to the 26 powers the states granted them. And only Laws. Laws duly passed by accountable legislators. The framers did not empower an unbridled, unaccountable administrative state to administer an auxiliary government. It was obvious and recognized by the framers that to implement the approved and delineated powers that are the framework that the Constitution provides that additional laws would necessarily be required and appropriate to establish governmental functions. There is no intellectually honest way to alternatively "interpret" this plain language. In fact, it needs no interpretation at all. How do you make such plain language "living and breathing"? Many people have heard of the necessary and proper clause, but considerably fewer know the rest of the statement, those in power would never point this out as it would impede their lawless and nefarious goals.

It now makes sense to look at the Necessary and Proper clause alongside the first clause of Article One Section Eight, the Taxing Clause, of Article One Section Eight which grants Congress the authority to tax, it states:

The Congress shall have Power To lay and collect Taxes, Duties, Imposts, and Excises, to pay the Debts and provide for the common Defence and general Welfare of the United States; but all Duties, Imposts and Excises shall be uniform throughout the United States.[11]

The Taxing clause is abused similarly to the Necessary and Proper clause by Congress and the courts and anti-constitutionalists in general. When this clause is appropriately viewed in context with the Necessary and Proper Clause, it is clear that Congress has the taxing authority to implement the powers that the states have ceded to the federal government, not the power to tax anything for any purpose.

I will provide two prime examples of using the Taxing clause inappropriately and unconstitutionally. The first example comes from the 1930s during the implementation of Franklin Roosevelt's New Deal. I encourage you to research this on your own as the details are fascinating. The short version of the story is that as the Roosevelt administration was seeking to enact Social Security, members of the administration were concerned that it would be struck down as unconstitutional (which it clearly is). The administration was advised by a sitting Justice, Justice Harlan Fiske Stone, that if Social Security were cloaked as a tax, then it would not have any constitutional issues with the high court. Justice Stone advised the administration that "The taxing power of the federal government, my dear; the taxing power is sufficient for everything you want and need." How can you possibly have a taxing authority that is broader than your clearly defined overall scope? You can't. The Taxing Clause does not grant plenary power to the government any more than does the Necessary and Proper Clause. It is critical to look at this clause though the lens of the states who granted the central government its limited powers. With the loud voices of the anti-federalists beckoning, the states would not have and did not grant such power to the central government.

My second example of an unconstitutional application of the Taxing Clause is the Affordable Care Act (AKA Obamacare). Justice Roberts also hid behind the government's authority to tax when the court ruled favorably on Obamacare. It is to me unfathomable that under a Constitution, such as ours, that goes to great pains to limit and control and delineate the powers of the central government that somehow, in one fell swoop, the government can take over approximately fifteen percent of the nation's economy.

If all we did as a country and as citizens was to retake control of the Constitution's Article One Section Eight and the unconstitutional application of the Taxing, Commerce, and Necessary and Proper clauses we would be a much freer and lawful republic.

So that's Article One, Section Eight of the Constitution, the totality of what the Congress can do. Let's move on to Article One, Section Nine a take a look and see the limits Congress put on itself.

The first clause of Article One, Section Nine addresses the issue of the importation of slaves and says that Congress cannot take up the issue until 1808. Clearly, slavery is our most egregious founding sin and flies in the face of *all men are created equal*. There is no excuse for one man to hold another in bondage. Period. But let us be clear, Great Britain brought slavery to the continent, Americans freed them.

The Migration or Importation of such Persons as any of the States now existing shall think proper to admit, shall not be prohibited by the Congress prior to the Year one thousand eight hundred and eight, but a Tax or duty may be imposed on such Importation, not exceeding ten dollars for each Person.[12]

Much of the remainder of Article One, Section Nine seeks to ensure the states that the central government will not be a heavy-handed one, again leery from the experiences under the crown. It continues to be evident that the delegates recognize that they need to sell the states and assuage their fears about this new form of government. And while there is no Bill of Rights in what is submitted to the states immediately following the convention, I believe that Article One, Section Nine is the closest thing to a Bill of Rights in the original document.

Article one Section Nine is proof that some of the framers intended to abolish slavery, although they put the issue off into the future by 20 years. While the central government had no standing on the subject of slavery within a state until the passage of the 13th amendment, they did have the authority to support a navy. With our navy, the U.S. government patrolled international waters from 1819 to 1862 (the date of the emancipation proclamation) to attempt to intercept slave ships headed to the western hemisphere. It is also important to note that the word slavery was not used in the Constitution, these were 'persons' being imported, a recognition of their divine spark.

Article One Section, Nine addresses issues related to legal rights, Habeas Corpus, cannot be suspended, so people cannot be held without cause. Bills of Attainder are forbidden, so laws cannot be passed declaring individuals guilty and punishing them without trial. And ex-post-facto laws are also not permitted, which declare an act illegal after an action has taken place. By having Article One (the Legislative Branch) deal with these issues which are closely tied to actions within the courts helps to solidify the concept that 'inferior' courts roll up to Congress.

Congress also says it will not play favorites with the states and commits to being good stewards of your money by limiting expenditures to those that have been duly appropriated. We also see Congress addressing the issue of states taxing one another and prohibiting themselves from taxing exports from the states as well. Lastly, Congress again embraces the idea that *all men are created equal* by forbidding titles of nobility and ensuring the states that people serving in government will not be corrupted by special treatment from foreign powers.

Section Ten is the last section in Article One, it places limits on the states. Article One, Section Ten is, by-and-large, a mirror of Article One, Section Nine, with those restrictions Congress placed on itself now placed onto the states. With the Constitution's separation of powers, checks and balances and the restrictions and limitations placed on both the federal and state governments it is not too difficult to see why the framers original submission to the states did not include a Bill of Rights and were initially resistant to including one as they believed sufficient clarity and limits were in place to protect the citizenry.

Article One, Sections Nine and Ten continue to evidence that the Constitution is not complicated, indecipherable, or irrelevant. The arguments by the anti-Constitutionalists regarding the Constitution's complexity are specious at best and quickly crumble when we take the time to read the plain text. Article One is easily the longest of the Constitution's seven Articles (roughly half of the entire document), yet as we have gone through it, we have seen no complexity and no outdated language or ideas. We have seen that it is logically and clearly organized, and we consistently see its roots and links that seek to codify the revolutionary ideas in the Declaration of Independence.

Someone is trying to pull the wool over our eyes. Sometimes there is actually truth. In today's society, we are taught that everyone's ideas are valid. No, they are not. We are indoctrinated with the notion that compromise is good; that bi-partisanship should be the goal. No, it should not; adherence to our principles and the rule of law should be the goal. Because the Constitution is a finite document any compromise can only pull us away from it, you can never get closer to it with compromise. This is why the anti-Constitutionalist always speaks in these terms of bipartisanship and compromise, he knows any compromise gets him closer to his ends. I had a colleague once tell me that it is the job of a "good lawyer" to expand the meaning of a law; I say that it is the job of all citizens, be they interested parties or not to seek the truth and adhere to our principles.

We'll move to Article Two, which describes the executive and the executive branch. Once we understand the structure, and intent of the executive branch we'll go through the current executive branch cabinet and see how it aligns with the 26 functions that gained legitimacy when the states agreed to centralize them.

CHAPTER 6:

ARTICLE TWO; THE EXECUTIVE BRANCH

~~~~~~~~~~~~~~~~~~~~~~~~~~~~~~~~~~~~~~~

Article Two contains four sections. Similar to Article One, Article Two begins with Section One laying out the method by which the President is elected, the term of office, qualifications for office, a plan for succession and how he is to be compensated. Within the methodology for electing the president, we continue to see the state's involvement as the president is chosen by electors selected by the states. Importantly, the smaller states put forward the notion of an Electoral College as a means to ensure that their voices would be heard in the election of the president. Today it is the larger states that complain about the Electoral College because they feel the small states have too much of a voice. When a country is borne from states, all the states consenting to Union will necessarily and obviously insist that they are still to be counted. Aspects of Article Two, Section One are later modified by amendment which later on we'll briefly discuss. We also see the famous oath of office in Article Two, Section One. :

"I do solemnly swear (or affirm) that I will faithfully execute the Office of President of the United States, and will to the best of my Ability, preserve, protect and defend the Constitution of the United States." [1]

Oaths matter. Words matter. The President, with his hand on a bible, swears this oath. He is about to be entrusted by the American people to honor this oath. The first word in the operative phrase of the oath is *'preserve.'* Preserve, not fundamentally change, not skirt, not ignore, not obstruct; preserve. If presidents have been faithfully preserving for the last 230 years, why are we so far afield?

Article Two, Section Two describes the responsibilities of the office of President. Not surprisingly, the duties are traceable back to Article One, Section, Eight's 26 centralized functions. The title of president is not chosen lightly. Given the desired separation of powers and the fact that we had recently thrown off a monarch, we certainly were not going to have a king. What was needed was someone to preside over the implementation of legitimate, necessary, and proper laws, passed by Congress and signed into law. The president will be the commander in chief of the armed forces, negotiate treaties, and establish the necessary departments to run the government. We are seeing that the president and the executive branch are the logical means by which laws will be implemented. We again see the system of checks and balances come into play whereby necessary appointments and treaties need to be confirmed by the senate as well as the establishment of an inferior class of officers to be determined by Congress that the president can directly hire. We further see checks and balances with the judiciary as it is the president who appoints Supreme Court Justices, who then, in turn, need to be confirmed by the senate. What don't we see? We don't see any of the complexity and inconsistency that the anti-Constitutionalist sees, I wonder why.

Article Two, Section Three is where we see the Constitutional requirement for the State of the Union address and the president also becomes the head of state when given the responsibility to receive foreign ministers officially. Article Two, Section Three, then makes it utterly unambiguous that the president is to implement duly passed laws through this clause:

he shall take Care that the Laws be faithfully executed,[2]

Neither Article Two Section, Three, nor the other sections reference the President's authority to use *a pen and a phone* to legislate from the executive branch, only to faithfully execute duly passed laws.

Article Two, Section Four describes how the president and all other civil officers are to be removed from office, by impeachment. Not by impeachment or some other way, just by impeachment. Currently, this issue is a giant can of worms that I believe will distract from my overall goal for the book, so I am not going to open that can.

So, Article Two in typically concise language, establishes the executive branch, the states accept that we will have a co-equal executive branch by their ratification of the Constitution and the states understand that the scope and the context of the executive branch is to faithfully execute laws pertaining to the 26 functions that the states said could be centralized. Let's look at today's cabinet and see how we are doing with the concepts of *faithful* and *preserve*. We'll compare the members of the president's current cabinet (as described on the White House website) to the original 26 governmental functions that Congress had jurisdiction over (per Article One Section Eight) and which the president would faithfully execute thereby preserving the Constitution.

Cabinet Member   Part of Approved Central Scope

Cabinet Member	Part of Approved Central Scope
Agriculture	No mention whatsoever
Commerce	Yes
Defense	Yes
Education	No mention whatsoever
Energy	No mention whatsoever
Health and Human Services	No mention whatsoever
Homeland Security	Yes
Housing and Urban Development	No mention whatsoever
Interior	No mention whatsoever
Labor	No mention whatsoever
State	Yes
Transportation	No mention whatsoever
Treasury	Yes
Veterans Affairs	Yes
Attorney General	Yes
White House Chief of Staff	Yes
Environmental Protection Agency	No mention whatsoever
Office of Management and Budget	Yes
United States Trade Representative	Yes
United States Mission to the United Nations	Yes
Small Business Administration.	No mention whatsoever

Not so good, of the twenty-Six members of the current cabinet, ten members that have no relationship to the original 26 legitimate functions of the federal government whatsoever. Of the sixteen legitimate tasks represented in the cabinet most, if not all have exceeded or bastardized the initial intent. We discussed at length the commerce clause and how, somehow, *among* means *within*. Of the legitimate departments most have overstepped their bounds as well but, how did the illegitimate cabinet members get there?

In addition to the takeaways that I have asked you to consider thus far of consistently looking back to our founding principles of *all men are created equal* and *consent of the governed* there is another critical concept that citizens need to be keenly aware of; *standing*. This is how standing works, the anti-Constitutionalist wants to take more power away from the states and the people. He knows he doesn't have the authority to assume these powers, but he does not care, and he views the amendment process as too high a hurdle (and for a good reason) as we will see when we get to article five.

Let's use the Department of Education as our example to demonstrate why standing is critical and the role it plays in establishing a new department and more generally how the anti-Constitutionalists ignore standing as a means to always be seizing power. Clearly, the founders were well educated men and knew of the necessity of an educated citizenry to understand their rights under the Constitution, yet the word education does not exist in the Constitution. Originally part of the Department of Health, Education and Welfare (none of which are among the 26 legitimate and delineated Congressional authorities) beginning in 1953, under a Republican Congress and Republican President Eisenhower. The Department of Education was spun out under Democratic President Jimmy Carter in 1979 and the Democrat-controlled Congress. Legislative machinations aside, what ends up happening in these debates is always the discussion around 'is this a good idea or a bad idea'? The conversation inevitably moves to an emotional argument, such as 'don't you think education is important'? (In my case, it is glaringly evident that not only does the federal government have no standing in education, but education is so important that I don't want the federal government anywhere near it.) People then debate the merits of education and of course if it's 'for the children' it must be a good idea. The media is a knowing coconspirator with their polls filled with leading questions that show the people's views that of course, we need the central government involved in education. However, the media will never mention that federal government involvement in education is not constitutionally permitted. So what is wrong with debating the merits of a proposal, it sure seems logical to weigh the pros and cons of any issue? The issue is that going straight to the emotional debate of the merits, the most critical step is skipped. We must always first ask, does the government have *standing* regarding the issue being proposed? The reason the anti-Constitutionalist skips this step is that he could not possibly care less about perceived limitations on his authority, he believes his power is plenary. Yet we now know there are only 26 legitimate functions that the states ceded to the federal government and that Congress can only pass laws that are necessary and proper for carrying into execution those laws and that the executive branches' purpose is to faithfully execute only those laws. We are losing our republic, in large part, because the citizenry does not insist on a debate regarding standing.

That is an example of just one department, at the department level. If we drill a bit deeper, it gets even worse. It is within these departments that house the scores of agencies and legions of bureaucrats that the Constitution is further shredded. We have departments who themselves are created illegitimately bureaucratically legislating without our consent and without standing and leaving us with little recourse to the tormenting tyrants.

All legislative Powers herein granted shall be vested in a Congress of the United States, which shall consist of a Senate and House of Representatives.[3] Really?

So what of checks and balances? I thought the executive was supposed to be one of the checks on the legislature, the founders knew that a legislature could become tyrannical just as a king could, that was the whole rationale for our system in the first place. I suggest that instead of one co-equal branch checking another they are in fact colluding. The near-complete absence of any discussion regarding the government's standing requires the citizenry to realize what is being done to them and insist that establishing whether or not the government has standing becomes a predicate act to discussing the merits of the proposal.

CHAPTER 7:

ARTICLE THREE; THE JUDICIAL BRANCH

~~~~~~~~~~~~~~~~~~~~~~~~~~~~~~~~~~~

Article Three of the Constitution defines the federal judiciary, and you can see the roots of an independent judiciary in the Declaration of Independence list of grievances:

He has made Judges dependent on his Will alone, for the tenure of their offices, and the amount and payment of their salaries.[1]

Article Three is broken down into three sections. Article Three, Section One, consistent with the beginning of Articles One and Two, clearly lays out the overarching responsibility of the judiciary, establishes the Supreme Court and recognizes Congress' role in establishing the inferior federal courts. Additionally, Article Three, Section One sets (by omission) the qualifications for judges establishes the term of their service and their compensation.

Article Three, Section Two defines the jurisdiction of the federal judiciary. With a clear and distinct link back to Article One, Section Eight's consented to legitimate governmental functions the jurisdiction (as I process it) is broken down into three areas. First, jurisdiction over all federal laws emanating out of the 26 legitimate governmental functions. Second, Article Three, Section Two claims jurisdiction over the multiple relationships that exist among the states and their citizens in a way that is reminiscent of the usage of the word *among* in Article One Section Eight's Commerce clause. The jurisdiction claimed in Article Three Section Two includes *between* two or more States; *between* a State and Citizens of another State,—*between* Citizens of different States,—*between* Citizens of the same State claiming Lands under Grants of different States, and *between* a State, or the Citizens thereof, and foreign States, Citizens or Subjects. The word *'between'* in Article Three, like *'among'* in Article One is to simply establish the federal judiciary as a referee where any other referee would be subject to bias. As an example, in a dispute between two states, clearly, the arbiter cannot be the judiciary of either of those states as neither is a neutral party. This clear role of the referee was not intended to empower the federal government with any regulatory authority within states or over their citizens.

And lastly, Article Three Section Two grants jurisdiction over cases between the United States and foreign governments and their ministers.

Article Three, Section Three defines treason:

Treason against the United States, shall consist only in levying War against them, or in adhering to their Enemies, giving them Aid and Comfort. No Person shall be convicted of Treason unless on the Testimony of two Witnesses to the same overt Act, or on Confession in open Court.[2]

The founders debated the scope of what would be considered treason, it was finally agreed that the scope of treason should be narrow. Today we are always hearing about this person or the other committing treason, almost none rise to the narrow scope the founders established. Clear, everyday language articulating to the states the role of the new federal judiciary, language, and structure consistent with the Constitution's first two Articles, rounding out the third of the co-equal branches. Nothing inconsistent, nothing indecipherable, nothing complex. And the succinctly stated primary role of the judiciary is its jurisdiction over:

> *The judicial Power shall extend to all Cases, in Law and Equity, arising under this Constitution, the Laws of the United States,[3]*

Naturally, the laws arising under this Constitution should be legitimate laws relating to functions for which the central government has been given jurisdiction, passed by Congress and signed into law by the president. However, if those laws are challenged as illegitimate, the co-equal Court will strike down the unjust law. Well, that's how it was supposed to happen. Instead, we have a third willing coconspirator effectively, or actually nullifying the Constitution. Activist judges continue to pull us away from the Constitution, some justices appear to truly despise the document, encouraging other countries to look to an alternative such as South Africa in the case of Justice Ruth Bator Ginsberg. Really, a Supreme Court justice disparaging our Constitution in favor of that of South Africa, and doing it on foreign soil. How is it that that is tolerated?

Yet we consistently hear from anti-Constitutionalist politicians and pundits in the media who are trying to dismantle our system of government that when a court ruling does not go their way (there are still occasions when this happens) that it is due to an activist judge or court on the "right." How, pray tell, can you be an activist judge by taking no action, by not moving away from the clear original intent? This is among their most inane and ludicrous arguments. I believe this is why the anti-Constitutionalist so aggressively focuses on case law as precedent as opposed to the original document. Anti-constitutionalists seek to uphold rulings that likely originate from an actual activist anti-Constitutionalist judge. When we stray from the original intent, and thereby the founding principle of *all men are created equal,* we stray onto dangerous ground. How can justice be served when laws, in the eyes of the anti-constitutionalist, have no firm-fixed meaning?

Moreover, an activist judge, who can only move away from the original intent, is violating the separation of powers by, in effect, crafting law and knowingly changing a law's meaning from the bench. As with most of the subjects that I touch on, there exist many excellent books on the runaway courts. My goal here is to simply show the clarity of the intent of the limitations placed on the federal government by the states, I believe that by showing the original intent you will likely come to the conclusion that I have, that the federal government has substantially exceeded its consented to authority.

CHAPTER 8:

ARTICLE FOUR; THE STATES

Onto Article Four. Article Four deals with the states and is broken down into four sections. The first part of Article Four Section One is referred to as the Full Faith and Credit Clause, its purpose to provide one of the necessary mechanisms to form a union out of multiple sovereign states. The Full Faith and Credit clause requires that the courts of one state will honor the rulings of the courts of another state.

Article Four, Section Two effectively establishes a common citizenry as people traveling from one state to another are not to be considered foreigners. The privileges and immunities they are granted are long-standing positive rights (as opposed to Natural rights) from British antiquity. This section also provides for criminal extraditions and the return of escaped slaves.

Several of the concepts in Article two have a direct trace back to the Articles of Confederation, helping to make the case that the Philadelphia convention was not hijacked and what emerged from the convention was a logical evolution of the Articles of Confederation.

Article Four, Section Three's roots can be seen in the Declaration of Independence grievances, where the crown restricted the geographic growth of the colonies.

He has endeavoured to prevent the population of these States; for that purpose obstructing the Laws for Naturalization of Foreigners; refusing to pass others to encourage their migrations hither, and raising the conditions of new Appropriations of Lands.[1]

Article Four, Section Three provides a method for adding new states and as is typical that process is checked by the applicable state legislature and Congress.

Article Four, Section Four guarantees a republican *form* of government. A republican form of government is one where the citizens' vote is heard either directly or through a representative, has no monarch, and is based on the rule of law. I believe that one of the most interesting parts of the Constitution is that the word democracy does not exist in the Constitution. Those unfamiliar with the document find this puzzling. We know the attributes of a republic, what then is a democracy? The confusion arises because a democracy can be both a *type* and *form* of government. As a type of government, a democracy means that broadly speaking the citizens vote periodically. America is a type of democracy that's *form* is republican. As a *form* of government, a democracy means majority rule. In a democratic *form* of government, the minority is at the whim of the majority, and therefore there is no recognition of your God-given, unalienable Natural Rights. I find the naming of the two major political parties in America interesting when looked at in this light.

CHAPTER 9:

ARTICLE FIVE; AMENDING THE CONSTITUTION AND MAINTAINING CONSENT

~~~~~~~~~~~~~~~~~~~~~~~~~~~~~~~~

Article Five of the Constitution describes how the Constitution can be amended. The Constitution can be amended in just two ways. An amendment can begin in Congress with a two-thirds vote of each house and then be ratified by three-quarters of the states. The president has no role in the process as the two-thirds vote by Congress represents a veto-proof majority. Alternatively, two-thirds of the states can convene to suggest amendments to be ratified by three-quarters of the states. Neither Congress nor the President has a role in the state-initiated process.

Article Five does not say that a statute can amend the Constitution, it does not mean that the Constitution can be amended by a President with a pen and a phone or by a judge who doesn't happen to like a law or the president.

Why has such a high hurdle been established to amend the Constitution? As we learned in Article Four, the founders were not fans of the "mob rule" created by a democratic *form* of government. When the framers crafted the Constitution, it represented their desire to institute a *form* of government to which all of society consented, thus, requiring the consent of at least nine of the thirteen states to ratify the document. Why, if the initial requirement is for roughly two-thirds of the states (9/13) to consent to make a society would they allow society to be changed with a simple majority of the legislature, the actions of a president or the ruling of a judge? They didn't, it would have been illogical and utterly inconsistent with everything they had done up until that point.

So, the first five articles of the Constitution show the formation of our three co-equal branches of government, the description of each branch, their roles, responsibilities, and the checks and balances placed among the three branches and between the central government and the states. Two straight forward methods to amend the Constitution are also described. The logical, clear, consistent, and simple formation of each article is plain to see, so what is this talk about a *living and breathing* Constitution, what does it mean and what are its origins?

To the anti-Constitutionalist, the idea of a *living breathing* Constitution means that the Constitution has no fixed meaning and in fact no meaning at all. This is the anti-Constitutionalist's primary tool to change our society without the necessary *consent of the governed*. A *living and breathing* Constitution does not recognize the fixed nature of the 26 original functions articulated in Article One, Section Eight, ceded to the central government by the states, nor does it accept the required societal consent as described in Article Five to add to, or subtract from that list by using one of the two methods of amendment. It means the government can do whatever it wants to you and that you have no natural rights, only rights granted to you from another man and no say in the matter. If the believer in a *living and breathing* Constitution believes he can grant you rights or take them away, he does not believe he is your equal, nor does he believe that *all men are created equal.* The anti-constitutionalist is the chief proponent for debating the merits of an idea (and then not even so much) and never acknowledging whether or not the government has standing in an issue as he believes his power knows no bounds. Through everything we have learned about the founder's clear intent and the consistent and logical approach by which they instituted the Constitution that for one to believe in a *living breathing* Constitution is simply intellectually dishonest. Let's learn a little bit more about the origins of a *living breathing* Constitution to dispel the legitimacy of this view further.

The notion of a *living and breathing* Constitution comes out of the progressive era. The progressive era in this country began in the late nineteenth century, and its devotees had some very nasty beliefs. They believed in eugenics, the belief that society can and should be improved upon by selective breeding (wow!). Margaret Sanger was one of these early progressives whose eugenic beliefs survive to this day through the organization she founded, Planned Parenthood. Women's reproductive rights, give me a break. Progressives did not believe in equality of the races or individual liberty or natural rights. They believed that the government could and should cure society's ills. Although there were progressives in government before Woodrow Wilson (including Teddy Roosevelt) I believe that Woodrow Wilson is the initial prime culprit in trying to nullify the Constitution by making it a *living and breathing* document. This quote is from Wilson's book published while he was running for president in 1912.

Society is a living organism and must obey the laws of life, not of mechanics; it must develop. All that progressives ask or desire is permission – in an era when 'development,' 'evolution,' is the scientific word

– to interpret the Constitution according to the Darwinian principle; all they ask is recognition of the fact that a nation is a living thing and not a machine." [1]

That is one messed up quote, and an entirely intellectually and morally bankrupt statement. Let's dismantle it. Society is not a living organism, society in America is an amalgamation of individuals proximate to one another who share common beliefs and morays. I say in America because I believe anyone who shares our beliefs can become American. Society in Europe is different in that the notion of society also requires a shared heritage. I don't believe you can become Swiss. Within the above quote, I believe this is actually Wilson giving himself unbridled authority:

"All that progressives ask or desire is permission." [2]

Well, Wilson never asked for permission to allow society to evolve; that would require getting consent from the governed by amending the Constitution. You cannot amend the Constitution by asking an ethereal question, such as 'May I have unbridled, complete authority to interpret the Constitution as I wish?' What Wilson did was a complete usurpation of power, taking power from the people and giving it to bureaucrats.

Furthermore, as we have learned, all laws come out of Congress, so Wilson's branch does not have the authority to legislate. Wilson, by this statement, shows he has no intention whatsoever to either *preserve* the Constitution or to *faithfully* execute just laws that have been duly passed. Wilson obviously knows the high Constitutional hurdle of getting society to consent to his whims through the amendment process so he asks his coconspirators in the legislative and judiciary to *interpret* the Constitution out of existence so he and his ilk can do whatever they want to you without your consent. A *living and breathing* Constitution is a dead Constitution, and the idea of one makes our government an arbitrary and tyrannical one.

To debate whether or not the Constitution is *living and breathing* is clearly completely illegitimate as the genesis of the idea is without merit. The intent of the founders was for the Constitution to have a fixed meaning with delineated powers, consented to by the governed, powers that embraced and protected natural rights and a precise methodology to amend the document as the society saw fit. The only way that the anti-Constitutionalist can get away with this behavior is to hope the public doesn't figure out the degree to which their republic has been stolen.

James Madison articulated his view of the necessity of a fixed meaning of the text of the Constitution this way in a correspondence with Richard Henry Lee, who we remember as the author of the Lee resolution which granted the colonies independence for Great Britain:

"I entirely concur in the propriety of resorting to the sense in which the Constitution was accepted and ratified by the nation. In that sense alone it is the legitimate Constitution.[3]

Madison is clearly calling upon the principles found in the Declaration of Independence by saying that the Constitution is only legitimate as it was consented to.

That to secure these rights, Governments are instituted among Men, deriving their just powers from the consent of the governed,[4]

However, none of the founders were saying the Constitution can't be changed, here is what Jefferson (who, as we know was not at the convention) says on the issue of the necessity of change to government:

"I am not an advocate for frequent changes in laws and Constitutions, but laws and institutions must go hand in hand with the progress of the human mind. As that becomes more developed, more enlightened, as new discoveries are made, new truths discovered and manners and opinions change, with the change of circumstances, institutions must advance also to keep pace with the times. We might as well require a man to wear still the coat which fitted him when a boy as civilized society to remain ever under the regimen of their barbarous ancestors."[5]

Jefferson fully recognized the need for societies to evolve, but not via the unchecked power of government. The anti-Constitutionalists use quotes like this to advocate for the progressives *living and breathing* Constitution, but Jefferson also said:

To take a single step beyond the text would be to take possession of a boundless field of power.[6]

And he said this:

On every question of construction carry ourselves back to the time when the Constitution was adopted, recollect the spirit manifested in the debates and instead of trying what meaning may be squeezed out of the text or invented against it, conform to the probable one in which it was passed[7]

I think it might be this quote that causes the anti-constitutionalist to claim they need a time machine. Regardless, in advocating for what Jefferson would call boundless power, the anti-Constitutionalist will show only the quote (and quotes like it) advocating for a changeable document without dealing with the clear necessity of an originalist interpretation and that the consent of the governed would always be required through an amendment process. The anti-Constitutionalist progressive simply wants your blanket permission to interpret (or ignore) the Constitution because he believes he knows better than you; he is not your equal, he is your master. It is not just that the anti-constitutionalist feels he knows better than you; he believes that that matters.

The framers clearly and naturally understood that the Constitution's meaning is fixed until amended. Why else would they include Article Five's amendment process? It is just that simple and obvious. The framers would never conceive of interpreting away all men are created equal or the requirement for consent of the governed. There is nothing whatsoever that would suggest they would. The anti-Constitutionalist deceitfully misconstrues the founder's advocacy for a changeable document, through an agreed-upon process, to mean they advocated for anarchy.

Currently, there is a movement underway to convene a Convention of the States (also referred to as an Article Five Convention) to consider certain amendments to the Constitution. This method of amending the Constitution has never been used to achieve any of the 27 amendments in the document. Almost nothing is talked about this process in the media, but it is gaining momentum, and at least a couple of dozen states of the 34 (two/thirds of the 50) states required have committed to participating. It was prescient for the founders to put this alternative amendment process in the Constitution, they realized that a legislature could become tyrannical and the states needed a check for that. Many of the changes to the limit the power of the central government, such as term limits, balanced budgets, and perhaps a state check against Supreme Court rulings, for which the states would advocate could be accomplished through an Article Five amendment process. Congress simply will not take up these amendments as they seek to limit the power of the central government. I, for one, believe this is a good idea as any amendment that comes out of the convention needs to be ratified by 38 (three/fourths) of the states which would evidence societal consent to the changes and make the process completely legitimate.

CHAPTER 10:

ARTICLES 6 AND 7; SUPREMACY, TREATIES, OATHS, AND RATIFICATION

~~~~~~~~~~~~~~~~~~~~~~~~~~~~~~~~~~~~

Article Six of the Constitution has a logical and straightforward purpose, consistent with the rest of the document; it serves to make a clarifying point that any law or treaty of the United States becomes the Supreme Law of the Land. With the narrow scope of the federal Constitution's 26 consented to functions the founders are making clear that although limited, those 26 functions are the purview of the central government. This simple article has similarity to portions of other articles (One and Three) in that it is structural and clearly laying out the jurisdiction that is to be ceded to the central government by the states. No complexity here either.

It is also in Article Six that we see the requirement for those in public service to take an oath to the Constitution, after being modified over the years today's oath (Supreme Court is slightly different) reads:

"I, _____, do solemnly swear (or affirm) that I will support and defend the Constitution of the United States against all enemies, foreign and domestic; that I will bear true faith and allegiance to the

same; that I take this obligation freely, without any mental reservation or purpose of evasion; and that I will well and faithfully discharge the duties of the office on which I am about to enter. So help me, God."[1]

With such a clear oath requiring fidelity to the Constitution, how can we have strayed so far? The answer is always the same in my estimation, we, as a people do not demand fidelity. When one is required to "bear true faith and allegiance," it certainly does not imply that the Constitution can be interpreted as one desires, including those in the courts. The ignorance of those in Congress to the contents of the Constitution is striking. How could they propose the laws they do if they were faithful to their oath? We have even heard politicians in recent times say they can pass any law whatsoever and it is up to the courts to determine the constitutionality of that law. This attitude serves to make my point that Congress does not take their oath of fidelity seriously.

Article Seven of the Constitution is even simpler than Article Six. However, it puts an exclamation point on the entire argument I have been attempting to make. Article Seven says that when nine, or roughly two/thirds, of the states, ratified the Constitution, the new government will go into place. I look at Article Seven as the act by which the federal government formally asks the states for consent to this new form of government. As we have learned the Constitution actually goes into place on March 4, 1789, after 11 states (the last two, North Carolina and Rhode Island followed shortly thereafter) ratify and George Washington is inaugurated President on April 30 1789.

CHAPTER 11:

THE FIRST TEN AMENDMENTS; THE BILL OF RIGHTS

We now have a new government, but there is unfinished business as the anti-federalists insisted that a Bill of Rights was necessary and needs to be taken up in the first Congress. Keeping their word, James Madison, now a Congressman from Virginia, introduced to Congress nine proposed articles of amendment on June 8, 1789. After a couple of months of debate the concepts in those nine amendments turned into twelve one sentence amendments (that's right, the first ten amendments of the Constitution are all just one clear and succinct sentence each!) that were agreed to be sent to the states on September 25, 1789 (they were officially sent on September 28). Of the twelve proposed amendments submitted to the states for ratification ten were ratified, and on December 15, 1791, they became the first ten amendments to the United States Constitution. Interestingly, it was amendments three through twelve that were ratified. Proposed Amendment One, regarding Congressional apportionment was never ratified and is still technically before the states. Proposed amendment two was finally ratified, but not until May 5, 1992 (that's right 1992). It dealt with pay increases for Congress. Let's look at the first ten amendments as ratified, The Bill of Rights:

Bill of Rights

*Congress of the United States

begun and held at the City of New-York, on Wednesday the fourth of March, one thousand seven hundred and eighty nine.

THE Conventions of a number of the States, having at the time of their adopting the *Constitution, expressed a desire, in order to prevent misconstruction or abuse of its powers, that further declaratory and restrictive clauses should be added: And as extending the ground of public confidence in the Government, will best ensure the beneficent ends of its institution. RESOLVED* by the Senate and House of Representatives of the United States of America, in Congress assembled, two thirds of both Houses concurring, that the following Articles be proposed to the Legislatures of the several States, as amendments to the *Constitution of the United States, all, or any of which Articles, when ratified by three fourths of the said Legislatures, to be valid to all intents and purposes, as part of the said Constitution; viz. ARTICLES* in addition to, and Amendment of the *Constitution of the United States of America, proposed by Congress, and ratified by the Legislatures of the several States, pursuant to the fifth Article of the original Constitution.*

Frederick Augustus Muhlenberg Speaker of the House of Representatives John Adams, Vice-President of the United States and President of the Senate.

*Attest, John Beckley, Clerk of the House of Representatives. Sam. A. Otis Secretary of the Senate. *On September 25, 1789, Congress transmitted to the state legislatures twelve proposed amendments, two of which, having to do with Congressional representation and*

Congressional pay, were not adopted. The remaining ten amendments became the Bill of Rights.

Amendment 1
Congress shall make no law respecting an establishment of religion or prohibiting the free exercise thereof, or abridging the freedom of speech or of the press, or the right of the people peaceably to assemble and to petition the government for a redress of grievances.

Amendment 2
A well-regulated militia being necessary to the security of a free state, the right of the people to keep and bear arms shall not be infringed.

Amendment 3
No soldier shall, in time of peace, be quartered in any house without the consent of the owner, nor in time of war but in a manner to be prescribed by law.

Amendment 4
The right of the people to be secure in their persons, houses, papers, and effects against unreasonable searches and seizures shall not be violated, and no warrants shall issue but upon probable cause, supported by oath or affirmation, and particularly describing the place to be searched and the persons or things to be seized.

Amendment 5
No person shall be held to answer for a capital or otherwise infamous crime unless on a presentment or indictment of a grand jury, except in cases arising in the land or naval forces, or in the militia, when in actual service in time of war or public danger; nor shall any person be subject for the same offense to be twice put in jeopardy of life or limb; nor shall be compelled in any criminal case to be a witness against

himself, nor be deprived of life, liberty, or property without due process of law; nor shall private property be taken for public use without just compensation.

Amendment 6
In all criminal prosecutions, the accused shall enjoy the right to a speedy and public trial by an impartial jury of the state and district wherein the crime shall have been committed, which district shall have been previously ascertained by law, and to be informed of the nature and cause of the accusation; to be confronted with the witnesses against him; to have compulsory process for obtaining witnesses in his favor; and to have the assistance of counsel for his defense.

Amendment 7
In suits at common law, where the value in controversy shall exceed twenty dollars, the right of trial by jury shall be preserved, and no fact tried by a jury shall be otherwise reexamined in any court of the United States than according to the rules of the common law.

Amendment 8
Excessive bail shall not be required, nor excessive fines imposed, nor cruel and unusual punishments inflicted.

Amendment 9
The enumeration in the Constitution of certain rights shall not be construed to deny or disparage others retained by the people.

Amendment 10
The powers not delegated to the United States by the Constitution, nor prohibited by it to the states, are reserved to the states respectively, or to the people.[1]

So what is it that the Bill of Rights does, and what is a right anyway? As we have briefly discussed, many of the federalists did not see the necessity for a Bill of Rights, in fact, several were quite suspicious of including one. Those with this view argued, for example, 'why would I need to make a statement in a Bill of Rights pertaining to the prohibition of establishing a state religion when no such power was mentioned in the 26 powers already ceded to the central government by the states'. The federalists further feared that simply including additional delineated items, even in prohibition, could be misconstrued as the central government having some standing on an issue. As for complexity in the Bill of Rights, I don't think there exists any whatsoever, each amendment is just one sentence long.

The most important aspect (and often misunderstood) is that the Bill of Rights does not grant any rights at all. One man granting another man rights would violate the founding principle of *all men are created equal*. My equal cannot grant me a right. The Bill of Rights simply *recognizes* some of our God-given unalienable rights, and that others exist. The Bill of Rights, generally and in several places specifically, put an exclamation point on the limited nature of the central government.

Let's think about what an unalienable right is. The concept of God-given unalienable rights found in the Declaration of Independence (Nature and Natures God) are then codified through the adoption of the Constitution, unalienable rights are a bedrock of the founding of the nation. I think about God-given unalienable rights in straightforward terms.

Unalienable rights are intrinsic liberties granted to you by God that create no countervailing *obligation* on another; Unalienable Rights are symmetrical, I have to recognize that same right in you that you recognize in me.

Here are a couple of examples. My *freedom of speech* places no obligation on you other than for you to let me speak. You don't have to provide me with a venue at which to speak or pay me a speaking fee, you don't even have to listen to me speak, and the converse is equally valid. Your speech places no obligation on me to provide you a venue or to listen to you, I just have to let you speak. The freedom to practice my religion is another example of an unalienable right, it places no obligation on you to build me a church or attend my services, and it is symmetrical as it places no such obligations on me toward your practice of religion, we simply recognize in each other the right to worship, or not, as we see fit. The anti-Constitutionalist hates the universal nature of God-given unalienable rights and instead he seeks to strip you of those rights and substitute them with whatever privileges he sees fit. The concept of freedom of speech is actually the freedom to believe what you want to believe and to think about what you want to think. Suppression of the freedom of speech is suppressing how people think, clearly not a business that a government should be in. As opposed to *God-given unalienable rights* the anti-Constitutionalist seeks, to burden you with, *government-mandated, unavoidable obligations*. Anti-constitutionalists are often heard maligning the Constitution by referring to it as a series of 'negative covenants.' What the anti-constitutionalist means by negative covenants is that the Constitution's purpose is to limit the government's power. We Constitutionalists, on the other hand, know that limiting the power of government is the best way to ensure your liberty. The Constitution does not make anyone do anything. To the elite, who know better than you, that is a terrible construct. What they would rather have a constitution do is "guarantee" certain "rights," such as health care or a minimum income or other wealth transfer schemes. We now know that these wealth redistribution schemes cannot be rights as they are actually asymmetrical obligations placed upon citizens and not the recognition of natural, God-given, unalienable rights.

Lack of government standing aside, let's look a bit more deeply at health care. How can health care possibly be an unalienable right? Certainly, you have an inalienable right to pursue healthcare as that places no obligation on me, nor does my pursuit of healthcare burden you with an obligation. But the right to be *provided* healthcare is an entirely different thing. For you to have the right to be provided healthcare, I must now be burdened with the obligation to provide it to you. And if I am providing you with healthcare you are likely not providing me healthcare making healthcare an asymmetrical "right." What about doctors? Do they have an obligation to provide service, who then would be a doctor? Oh, I know, the government will then have to make people go to medical school to provide the service, just look at the former Soviet Union. Feel good ideas such as "free healthcare" will have utterly disastrous outcomes. Healthcare is not a "right," healthcare is a product.

Similarly, free college cannot be an inalienable right either. The asymmetrical nature of such a program provides one citizen with a benefit and another with an obligation. Oh, and not only are the merits of ideas like this ludicrous and violative of our founding principles but the central government, absent Constitutional amendment has no standing in either healthcare or education.

When I look at the Bill of Rights I see the identical logic and approach that we saw previously in the structure of both the Declaration of Independence and the Constitution. A clear preamble setting the purpose and the context of what is to follow and then laying out the individual amendments (they originally referred to the amendments as Articles e.g., Article the First, we'll just call them amendments) with clear ties back to our founding principles contained within the Declaration of Independence and the Constitution. Let's go through the amendments with an eye to their origins, the founding principles they support and the limits they place on the central government. We will also give them a simple test to see if they are unalienable, with no obligation other than mutual recognition.

The First Amendment recognizes five rights inferred in the Declaration of Independence and it emphasizes that even though Article One Section Eight (the things Congress can do) of the Constitution does not state the following in the affirmative or Article One Section Nine (the things Congress can't do) in the negative we are now explicitly stating the federal government has no standing to impede these specific liberties that is recognized in its citizen it states:

> *Congress shall make no law respecting an establishment of religion or prohibiting the free exercise thereof, or abridging the freedom of speech or of the press, or the right of the people peaceably to assemble and to petition the government for a redress of grievances.*[2]

Let's go through each of the rights that are recognized in the First Amendment. The framers start with a "negative covenant" by clarifying that there will be no state church such as Henry VIII's Church of England, the Anglican Church, the remnants of which are today's Episcopal Church. Interestingly, and not surprisingly the anti-Constitutionalist's favorite phrase on the subject of religion, *Separation of Church and State,* does not appear in the Bill of Rights or anywhere in the Constitution or the Declaration of Independence for that matter. That phrase was plucked out of obscurity from a letter written by Jefferson a decade after the ratification by an activist judge almost one hundred years later. The plain language of the clause needs no interpretation and does not require the government to place a wall between itself and religion, the central government simply can't form a religion. The anti-constitutionalist uses the phrase "separation between church and state" as a method to limit religion's role in society and to raise government itself to the level of a religion. The anti-constitutionalist cannot tolerate an entity (God) to be above them, so they attempt to strike down religion, and because of our Judeo Christian founding, Christianity in particular. Interestingly while the anti-constitutionalist won't let us hang the Ten Commandments in the public square as he ridiculously believes that that act is somehow establishing a religion, he will literally (and I know what literally means) let the government be the only way by which religion is established. How so? In the United States religions are established by recognition in the IRS code! I thought the language in the Constitution was clear that '*Congress shall make no law respecting an establishment of religion*' yet instead of an all-out ban on the government establishing religion we have the only means by which a religion is established is through the government. Crazy!

What is important in the Clause's typically careful wording here is that they are not recognizing your freedom *from* religion in the public square as the anti-constitutionalist will have you believe, the framers are recognizing your freedom *of* religion. Your freedom to practice your religion as you choose places no obligation on me nor mine on you. An official state religion (of which there are apparently many as recognized in the IRS code) would infringe on that right. Anti-Constitutionalists argue that the framers were deists and that the founding was a purely secular one. This is another typically specious argument from the anti-Constitutionalist because whether the framers were Christians or deists the argument is a distinction without a difference. There can be no doubt that all of the framers and founders believed that their unalienable rights could not and did not come from man, that our rights were bestowed upon us by the Creator.

Next, the freedom of speech is recognized in the First Amendment; *or abridging the freedom of speech*[3]

This quintessentially American freedom is core to our liberty. The freedom of speech certainly has all of the attributes of an unalienable right placing no obligation on anyone and existing with perfect symmetry for all citizens. Ben Franklin said this about the freedom of speech:

> "*Whoever would overthrow the liberty of a nation must begin by subduing the freeness of speech.*"[4]

We live in dangerous times regarding censorship of speech, particularly conservative speech. Academia, once an environment for the free exchange of ideas now abhors free speech and demands uniformity. Attempts to regulate speech are, in essence, attempts to regulate your thoughts, the anti-constitutionalists want to control how you think! Those in academia believe they have the right to grant or deny your free speech. They clearly do not believe that *all men are created equal* because equals cannot bestow rights on or remove rights from one another. Those who censor speech use terms like hate speech, offensive speech, or protected speech to rationalize their stance. But hate speech is speech, and the freedom of speech shall not be abridged. Is the word abridged ambiguous? Furthermore, not only do these people have no standing to abridge my speech, but their rationale itself forms a circular reference. By someone saying my speech is hate speech, they themselves are making offensive speech to me, the logic is lost on them. Or more likely, they are keenly aware but will use any means necessary to gain the uniformity of thought they desire. Dangerous stuff.

Another real-time threat by the anti-constitutionalist to the freedom of speech is federal prosecution for lying. Recently we have seen high profile figures such as Lt. General Michael Flynn prosecuted for lying to the FBI. In a society with a constitutionally recognized freedom of both speech and the right to not self-incriminate (we'll get to this in the Fifth Amendment), how is it that lying to the FBI can be a crime? The burden of proof for an alleged crime is on the government. To prosecute an individual for lying during an investigation absent the government bringing charges for the underlying crime is nothing short of Stalinesque. In this case, the government can't even necessarily tell which of the stories is true, they just know they are not the same, so they go after you for the discrepancy as a way to lever you into their desired position. This is an egregious case of people not being treated equally under the law and further proof that the anti-constitutionalist does not believe that all men are created equal. The FBI (federal prosecutors) are relatively unique in possessing this leverage over individuals, local police typically don't have this power. Why just the FBI. Do you think for a second that the FBI is always truthful when dealing with you during the investigation, isn't an inalienable right symmetrical? Who goes after the FBI for lying to the accused during an investigation? If we are going to make lying a crime (and I absolutely believe we should not) then shouldn't it always be a crime? I don't have an obligation to help make a legal case against me. The case against me should be made absent of my input. If we are all created equal, then the standard should be applied universally. Barack Obama infamously and knowingly lied to the public with his "if you like your healthcare, you can keep your healthcare" line. Congress has actually exempted itself from having to tell the truth on the floor of Congress. If Michael Flynn is prosecuted for lying, then most of the Congress should be too. The president, on the other hand, should be impeached when he lies as he is constitutionally exempted from criminal prosecution while in office. Instead, I say lying should not be a crime, people should always be aware that people have agendas, and they may be trying to advance their agenda, whatever it is.

The First Amendment also recognizes the freedom of press; *or of the press,*[5]

The framers certainly didn't need to belabor a point. There is not a tremendous amount of information on the origins of the necessity of a free press, but what does exist is completely consistent with other rights that are recognized and the intent of the Constitution more generally. Freedom of the press meets my test for an unalienable right as it creates no obligations on anyone and is symmetrical. As to its specific purpose, the founders believed the press to be yet another check on government whereby wayward officials could be compelled to good behavior by tenacious journalists.

Today much is said about the press and its bias. I believe that the press is biased. I believe that the press has always been biased and always will be. I also believe that every single person on earth is biased. I know I am biased. To have no bias is to have no opinion. I think it more relevant to ascertain the nature of the bias than dismiss an idea simply because of bias. My bias is to get to the original intent of the framers and therefore, what I believe is the only legitimate government. The one we consented to and the one we must continue to consent to. With a keen understanding of original intent, we, the citizens, can check both the government and the press. That is why it is crucial in a republic that the citizenry be educated, and certainly not educated by the government as that would provide no check whatsoever.

We hear the press today criticize those who call them fake news, the press is free to report as they wish, that is their right, however, those who they criticize also have the right to speak their mind, the symmetry between the press, the government and the citizenry. Furthermore, those who criticize are not threatening to shut down the press, which clearly would be an infringement, yet the press desires to silence voices critical to them. Criticizing the press in no way infringes on the press as that would make the freedom of speech an asymmetrical right where you can criticize me, and I can't criticize you. When the press accuses the current administration of being Nazis or Fascists, they must not know their history because if the administration were Fascist, the journalists would have long ago been dealt with.

To me, this issue of bias in the press is closely tied to the issue I described of debating the merit of an issue without first debating standing. The press can get people to see that there are 'two sides to and issue' and that 'we should compromise.' This logical but sinister argument takes advantage of an uninformed citizenry and can only serve to have us compromise away our principles. We can attribute four words to press freedom in the entire Constitution, none of those words require press conferences, access to officials, or a requirement to take questions from officials. The press today is fake news, it likely always has been fake news and it likely will always be fake news; the only way the citizenry will keep the press in check is to know why it is fake news.

The First Amendment also recognizes the right to assembly and petition the government regarding grievances;

> *or the right of the people peaceably to assemble and to petition the government for a redress of grievances*[6]

We'll deal with these last two rights in the First Amendment together and then I have an interesting and likely unpopular perspective. First, both the right to assemble and the right to petition the government over grievances meet my test of an unalienable right as they create no counterparty obligation and the right to free association is symmetrical, while the notion of symmetry is not relevant when with petitioning the government regarding grievances. The right to assemble was viewed by some of the framers as superfluous because if you have a right to speech, you must necessarily have to gather to speak, but the delineated right made it into the amendment regardless. The roots of the right to petition the government over grievances have quite a bit more substance behind it. Given their (mostly) English lineage, the founders and framers were aware that this was not always a right under the crown. It wasn't until the late seventeenth century that Englishmen could petition the crown. The overarching founding principle of *consent of the governed* can be clearly seen in this delineated right as in 'if I don't consent then you're going to hear about it'. The right to petition the government over grievances is also consistent with '*all men are created equal*' because if the nation's true power is vested in the people, surely they can voice grievances to their peers (their equals) represent the interests of the citizens.

When I think about these two rights, I often consider them along with the freedom of speech. In that context, one much-maligned profession seems to be very well represented in the First Amendment, the dreaded lobbyist. A lobbyist typically represents an association of some sort, a group of people who have freely assembled for some purpose. That group would like its representative to speak to the government regarding some issue of concern. I am no special pleader for lobbyists. But it seems to me that if I have the right to petition the government over grievances that it is not me who is the problem. If I am asking for some special favor that is not for the benefit of the general welfare or if I am asking the government to overstep its clear (to me) bounds in some way, that is my right, I can ask for anything I care to. The problem is with elected representatives (or unelected bureaucrats) being influenced by lobbyists; those representatives who either don't know or don't care about the limits placed upon government. If we wish to reduce the number of lobbyists and their influence, we need to insist on fidelity to the Constitution by our elected representatives. Were this to happen, K street rents would drop precipitously.

The Second Amendment, similar to the First Amendment says that even though the government never said it could restrict the right to bear arms or specifically that it couldn't (in Article One, Sections Eight and Nine), we are saying here, explicitly, that the central government has no standing in the issue. As is the case with all unalienable rights, the Second Amendment places no counter-party obligation and is completely symmetrical. I have the God-given, unalienable right to defend myself (be it from intruders or a tyrannical government) and you have the right to defend your-self, and there is no overt requirement to be armed. The Second Amendment states:

> *A well-regulated militia being necessary to the security of a free state, the right of the people to keep and bear arms shall not be infringed.*[7]

You may be aware that there is some controversy regarding our Second Amendment. I find the controversy completely intellectually dishonest. The anti-Constitutionalist uses his tried and true method of only debating the merits of his case and never addressing the issue of standing. There is all of this discussion regarding militias and commas, and it is all nonsense. What was it that the founders and framers believed was the primary purpose of having a gun? They believed that the gun's primary purpose was that it was to be used against tyrants. Period. Jefferson said:

> *"What country can preserve its liberties if their rulers are not warned from time to time that their people preserve the spirit of resistance. Let them take arms."*[8]

Jefferson also said:

> *"The Constitution of the United States (and of most of our states) assert that all power is inherent in the people; that they may exercise it by themselves, that it is there right and duty to be at all times armed"*[9]

Anti-federalist George Mason said:

> *"To disarm the people...[i]s the most effectual way to enslave them."*[10]

Noah Webster agreed with this sentiment by saying:

> *"Before a standing army can rule, the people must be disarmed, as they are in almost every country in Europe. The supreme power in America cannot enforce unjust laws by the*

sword; because the whole body of the people are armed, and constitute a force superior to any band of regular troops."[11]

Patrick Henry voiced his view this way:

Guard with jealous attention the public liberty. Suspect everyone who approaches that jewel. Unfortunately, nothing will preserve it but downright force. Whenever you give up that force, you are ruined.... The great object is that every man be armed. Everyone who is able might have a gun."[12]

Jefferson also recognized the value of firearms as sport saying:

"A strong body makes the mind strong. As to the species of exercises, I advise the gun. While this gives moderate exercise to the body, it gives boldness, enterprise and independence to the mind. Games played with the ball, and others of that nature, are too violent for the body and stamp no character on the mind. Let your gun therefore be your constant companion of your walks." – [13]

The founders also recognized the necessity of a militia, which is related to our right to assembly. Effectively every man was assumed to be the militia.

Richard Henry Lee said this regarding militia:

A militia when properly formed are in fact the people themselves...and include, according to the past and general usuage of the states, all men capable of bearing arms... "To preserve liberty, it is essential that the whole body of the people always possess arms, and be taught alike, especially when young, how to use them."[14]

And Elbridge Gerry put it this way:

What, Sir, is the use of a militia? It is to prevent the establishment of a standing army, the bane of liberty .... Whenever Governments mean to invade the rights and liberties of the people, they always attempt to destroy the militia, in order to raise an army upon their ruins."[15]

Alexander Hamilton presents a thorough argument by stating that:

If the representatives of the people betray their constituents, there is then no resource left but in the exertion of that original right of self-defense which is paramount to all positive forms of government, and which against the usurpations of the national rulers, may be exerted with infinitely better prospect of success than against those of the rulers of an individual state. In a single state, if the persons intrusted with supreme power become usurpers, the different parcels, subdivisions, or districts of which it consists, having no distinct government in each, can take no regular measures for defense. The citizens must rush tumultuously to arms, without concert, without system, without resource; except in their courage and despair."[16]

And certainly, the founders recognized that firearms are inherently dangerous. Jefferson put it this way:

"I prefer dangerous freedom over peaceful slavery."[17]

And Franklin more famously said:

They that can give up essential liberty to obtain a little tempo-rary safety deserve neither liberty nor safety."[18]

Sorry for all of the quotes. So all of the issues surrounding the "gun control" debate were understood in the time of the founding. They recognized the role of firearms in self-defense, and sport and in securing our liberties. Let's first talk about the federal government's standing regarding firearms. As we have seen with the quotes above, the overarching concern necessitating the right to bear arms was as a check to a potentially tyrannical government. So if your primary concern is a tyrannical government, would you then contemplate allowing that same government to have control of the means by which you protect yourself? Of course not. And they did not. The gun-grabbing anti-constitutionalist uses arguments such as 'well weapons today are much more powerful, so we must "regulate" or ban "military-style assault weapons." The weapons owned by the founders were the assault weapons of their day. How does technological evolution allow the usurpation of authority without the *consent of the governed*? The government has no authority to change a Constitutional amendment by statute, with or without technological advancement. And as to the insistence that this is a right of militias, I say OK. The militia is the people, and again if you are concerned about tyrants why would you give the potential tyrant the right to regulate your militia, that would not be much of a check, would it? In fact, as we see in our discussion regarding the Declaration of Independence, we would likely never have sought our independence if not for the extremely heavy-handed attempt to regulate our firearms and militia on the April day in 1775. Lastly, as it pertains to the dangers of guns in society as an excuse to strip rights away from citizens, this too is an illegitimate reason to usurp rights. The argument is that bad guys have guns, so let's take them away from the good guys, this is pure fantasy. Some people like to assume that somehow we all will be safer if we just got rid of guns. And while it doesn't happen every time a society is disarmed, every genocide occurs in a disarmed society. Do you think that the citizens of Turkey, the USSR, Germany, China, Cambodia, and others thought there would be mass exterminations? Of course not or they wouldn't have turned over their guns. For those who like to nullify the Constitution because they say the founders and framers were slaveholders (we'll get to this in the reconstruction era amendments) consider this; would a slaveholder give his slave a gun? What then is a man who prohibits another man from owning a gun; and what is a man that is prohibited from owning one?

Recently there has even been an argument against the necessity of an armed citizenry because the central government has "nukes". Well, first of all, thanks for the threat, secondly, I would like to point you to a little conflict called the Viet Nam War. The U.S had (but obviously did not use) nuclear weapons yet lost the conflict to an arguably inferior primarily guerilla force, the Viet Cong. It seems to me that threats of nuking the populous serve to strengthen the people's argument for keeping our guns. This too will be lost on the anti-constitutionalist.

Lastly, on the issue of firearms, the anti-constitutionalist love guns. If the citizenry does not comply with laws, legitimate or otherwise the anti-constitutionalist will knock on your door at 5AM with guns drawn to enforce their schemes. The deadly force possessed by the state is the only way to gain your cooperation, and the anti-constitutionalist does not want that force to be opposed.

The Third Amendment to the Constitution has a direct link to the principle of *consent of the governed* found in the Declaration of

Independence and Jefferson's list of grievances contained therein where he listed the following among them:

For Quartering large bodies of armed troops among us:[19]

After the Boston Tea Party, the British began housing troops in the resident's homes without their consent, infuriating them apparently enough so that the concept was specifically prohibited in the third amendment, it reads:

> *No soldier shall, in time of peace, be quartered in any house without the consent of the owner, nor in time of war but in a manner to be prescribed by law.*[20]

I also think about this amendment as being consistent with the others in that this notion was not included either Article One Section Eight or Nine so for clarity purpose and to appease the anti-federalists it was included. The Third Amendment also infers property rights. There has been almost no debate in the courts regarding the Third Amendment. There is occasional discussion around it being outdated, but a red flag goes up when I hear these discussions. First, so what if it is outdated? The fact that this has not yet been an issue in our republic does not mean it never will be. However, my more significant concern is that the nefarious among us could attempt to legislate away a never used amendment as a pathway to do the same with other amendments.

The Fourth Amendment, unlike the Third, is among the most litigated parts of the Constitution as it is relevant in every arrest that takes place, and it extends to your treatment at airports and beyond. The Fourth Amendment says:

> *The right of the people to be secure in their persons, houses, papers, and effects against unreasonable searches and seizures shall not be violated, and no warrants shall issue but upon probable cause, supported by oath or affirmation, and particularly describing the place to be searched and the persons or things to be seized.*[21]

While the courts continue to evolve their view, I think that the Fourth Amendment's original intent is quite straight forward and the structure of the sentence itself is consistent with language throughout the founding documents. The Fourth Amendment begins with a declaratory statement recognizing your unalienable right to be secure in your *person, houses, papers, and effects against unreasonable searches and seizures.* Importantly this clause further recognizes in a very assumptive fashion, property rights. The second part of the sentence then says 'to help ensure reasonableness, to be searched there needs to be probable cause and a specific warrant.'

The Fourth Amendment is seeking to solve a problem that John Adams, the primary author of the Fourth Amendment, believed to be the actual spark of the revolution (not the war). The issue was around the crown, in an attempt to quell smuggling instituted Writs of Assistance. Basically warrantless searches. Adams said this:

> *When I look back to the Year 1761, and recollect the Argument concerning Writs of Assistance, in the Superiour Court, which I have hitherto considered as the Commencement of the Controversy, between Great Britain and America, and run through the whole Period from that Time to this, and recollect the series of political Events, the Chain of Causes and Effects, I am surprized at the Suddenness, as well as Greatness of this Revolution. Britain has been fill'd with Folly, and America*

with Wisdom, at least this is my Judgment.—Time must determine.[22]

Again we see the Constitution logically trying to prevent problems the colonists experienced under the heavy-handed rule of the crown. The legal complexity that this amendment has turned into, I believe turns on the notion of reasonableness, which is not strictly definable other than through a common-sense test. So unlike other parts of the Constitution that the anti-Constitutionalist tries to undermine, I think it is 'reasonable' for two honorable people to have differing views on what is reasonable.

The Fifth Amendment to the Constitution is also what I view as a clarifying amendment. The lack of inclusion or exclusion of essential principles in Article One Sections Eight or Nine made the wary anti-federalists insist on the concepts in the Fifth Amendment, it provides for certain legal protections they wanted to be made explicit and its roots too can be seen in the list of grievances from the Declaration of Independence. It reads:

No person shall be held to answer for a capital or otherwise infamous crime unless on a presentment or indictment of a grand jury, except in cases arising in the land or naval forces, or in the militia, when in actual service in time of war or public danger; nor shall any person be subject for the same offense to be twice put in jeopardy of life or limb; nor shall be compelled in any criminal case to be a witness against himself, nor be deprived of life, liberty, or property without due process of law; nor shall private property be taken for public use without just compensation.[23]

The Fifth Amendment starts by ensuring an accused there is a legitimate case against him as that case has been vetted by his peers. This vetting is done through the English common law practice of a grand jury whereby a prosecutor makes his case to a group of citizens. In revolutionary times, the grand jury was often used to frustrate the crown as grand juries often resisted issuing indictment referrals on cases resulting from unpopular English laws. Today, the grand jury as a protection is quite limited and really best serves the prosecutor given the one-sided nature of these proceedings. The amendment then states an exception for the military which is in keeping with those affairs being enumerated in Article One, Section Eight. The Fifth Amendment is also where we see the double jeopardy clause, a long-standing principle of English common law which prevents someone, once found not guilty, from being repeatedly charged for the same crime, or the guilty of receiving multiple guilty verdicts for the same crime. The often heard 'I plead the fifth' come from the Fifth Amendments block on self-incrimination. As it pertains to the self-incrimination clause of the Fifth Amendment, why if I have the right to incriminate myself and if I have the freedom of speech, is it a crime to lie to the FBI? The FBI has shown recently and repeatedly their overzealousness in utilizing this abuse of power in attempting to secure indictments. Lying to the government should be the government's problem. I thought the purpose of this clause was to prevent self-incrimination; instead, the FBI completely ignores that principle, and they secure indictments for lying alone.

It is in the Fifth Amendment that we see the long-standing (dating back to the Magna Carta) right of due process recognized. Due process simply means you have the right to go to court to have your case heard. Many state Constitutions had similar provisions by the time the Bill of Rights is ratified.

Then we get to the takings clause. We have been taught that the takings clause is about eminent domain, the "right" of the government to take your property under certain circumstances. And it is, but I think there is much more here. Let's connect the dots back to the founding and the Declaration of Independence's principles. From a founding and originalist perspective, I think this is not just about real property. When the founding principles are applied, the world looks a little different.

We hold these truths to be self-evident that all men are created equal, that they are endowd by their Creator with certain unalienable Rights, that among these are Life, Liberty and the pursuit of Happiness[24]

Life, Liberty, and the pursuit of happiness; aren't these then my property? I have the right to work hard to achieve my life's goals, to gain my property. Why else would I work so hard? This property, the fruits of my labor cannot be taken away from me, certainly not by my equal or without my consent. Yet today we live in a massive redistributive welfare state, how'd that happen? There certainly should have been another amendment passed through which consent was earned to take my property and be denied just compensation. Don't hold your breath. There is no provision in any way, shape or form that allows the government to give your property to someone else, without just compensation and without your consent. Let's look at a few examples. You're taxed to pay the wage of a soldier in the 101st Airborne Division, well defense is one of the 26 enumerated powers, and you get something for it, so I say that's perfectly legitimate. How about your taxes paying the wage of someone in the Department of Education? Well, you get something for your money, it's just that I never asked for it or consented to it, that's bad. How about your tax dollar going to food stamps? Well, I get nothing in return, and I never consented to it, that's very bad. So apparently your government takes your most basic inalienable rights, your right to toil to achieve your life's desires and strips that away from you without your consent or compensation. Some people pay a third or more of their income to the federal government, of that two-thirds (or thereabouts) for illegitimate purposes. There is a word for taking someone's labor without their consent. Let's see what the founders said about the subject.

Madison said:

> *Government is instituted to protect property of every sort; as well that which lies in the various rights of individuals, as that which the term particularly expresses. This being the end of government, that alone is a just government which impartially secures to every man whatever is his own"*[25]

And this:

> *"the government of the United States is a definite government, confined to specified objects. It is not like the state governments, whose powers are more general. Charity is no part of the legislative duty of the government."*[26]

And this:

> *"I cannot undertake to lay my finger on that article of the Constitution which grants a right to Congress of expending, on objects of benevolence, the money of their constituents."*[27]

I think that is remarkably unambiguous. Why do the anti-Constitutionalists struggle so much with these simple principles? Jefferson felt similar to Madison, saying:

> *"A wise and frugal government, which shall leave men free to regulate their own pursuits of industry and improvement, and shall not take from the mouth of labor the bread it has earned — this is the sum of good government."*[28]

And this:

> *I predict future happiness for Americans if they can prevent the government from wasting the labors of the people under the pretense of taking care of them."*[29]

And this:

> *"Congress has not unlimited powers to provide for the general welfare, but only those specifically enumerated."*[30]

Franklin too echoed these sentiments, in his own style, saying:

> *"I am for doing good to the poor, but I differ in opinion of the means. I think the best way of doing good to the poor, is not making them easy in poverty, but leading or driving them out of it."*[31]

And this: *"The Constitution only gives people the right to pursue happiness. You have to catch it yourself."*[32]

I simply do not understand how the original intent could be any more clear on this issue, there is no standing whatsoever for the government to take your property and give it to someone else yet it is virtually *all* that government does today. Franklin was prescient when he said:

> *When the people find that they can vote themselves money, that will herald the end of the republic.*"[33]

The Sixth amendment expands upon the rights of the accused, it reads:

> *In all criminal prosecutions, the accused shall enjoy the right to a speedy and public trial by an impartial jury of the state and district wherein the crime shall have been committed, which district shall have been previously ascertained by law, and to be informed of the nature and cause of the accusation; to be confronted with the witnesses against him; to have compulsory process for obtaining witnesses in his favor; and to have the assistance of counsel for his defense.*[34]

The clauses in the Sixth Amendment can also be traced back to the grievances listed in the Declaration of Independence. For example:

> *For depriving us in many cases, of the benefits of Trial by Jury:*[35]

And:

> *For transporting us beyond Seas to be tried for pretended offences*[36]

The link to the principles of the Declaration of Independence is clear and undeniable. After dethroning the king and establishing the republic, the founders wanted to be sure that through sound structuring of the new government they could limit the possibility of governmental abuses such as those they experienced under the crown. So they made it completely clear that you have the right to a speedy trial by jury in the district that you were accused, you know with what and by whom you are being accused, the accused gets witnesses on his behalf and that you have the right to counsel. The recognition of these rights, if actually observed by the government, will make it much more difficult to unjustly convict an accused. Incidentally, the right to counsel clause, while not explicitly referenced as a grievance in the Declaration of Independence, was trying to solve for another abuse by the crown whereby they would often block the use of counsel by an accused. The original intent of the recognition of the right of the accused to counsel was simply access, not for it to be paid for by taxpayers, that didn't come about for another 150 years.

The Seventh Amendment addresses one of the more contentious, yet simple arguments brought by the anti-federalists during the ratification debates for the original Constitution. Actually, the absence of a guaranteed trial by jury in civil cases led several prominent founders to not consent to the original Constitution until the concept of a Bill of Rights was agreed to. The Seventh Amendment reads:

In suits at common law, where the value in controversy shall exceed twenty dollars, the right of trial by jury shall be preserved, and no fact tried by a jury shall be otherwise reexamined in any court of the United States than according to the rules of the common law[37]

The typically simple and clear language needs no interpretation. The Seventh Amendment also logically flows from the Fifth and Sixth Amendments which recognize (largely) the right of the accused in a *criminal* case and the Seventh then follows on to include *civil* cases as well. The concern that people should have about simple passages like the Seventh Amendment is that the anti-Constitutionalist requires that only selective sections of the Constitution (or the law) be upheld or enforced, with that arbitrary approach who knows what they will nullify or legislate away next.

The Eighth Amendment naturally and logically now flows from the preceding amendments by describing what happens if you are actually accused, it says:

> *Excessive bail shall not be required, nor excessive fines imposed, nor cruel and unusual punishments inflicted.*[38]

The history of the Eighth Amendment principles can be traced to the English Bill of Rights of the late 17th century and later the Virginia Declaration of Rights. The practice prior to the English Bill of Rights was sometimes bail was set so high as to effectively suspend habeas corpus. The principle also has roots in the Magna Carta's notion that the punishment should fit the crime.

Taken in total, the Fourth through Eighth Amendments recognize the rights of the accused. All of these are entirely in keeping with the Declaration of Independence's concept of *all men are created equal*, equal men cannot torment each other under the law, these amendments codify that concept.

The Ninth Amendment tries to accomplish the delicate balance of what is viewed as a danger of enumeration. The concern was that if certain items were enumerated, it would be perceived that all other items were excluded. It says:

> *The enumeration in the Constitution of certain rights shall not be construed to deny or disparage others retained by the people.*[39]

The debate about the enumeration of rights was one of the reasons that the framers didn't include a Bill of Rights in the original Constitution in the first place. What is consistent and clear in the Ninth amendment is that the founders, whether federalist or anti-federalist, all wanted to be sure the federal government was a limited one. The federalists were wary about the implications of enumeration while the anti-federalists, who were at least as wary, insisted on enumeration to which the Ninth Amendment would serve as a safeguard. Today the anti-Constitutionalist will use this amendment to claim rights that do not meet the standard of an unalienable right, rights that do not impose an obligation on a fellow citizen and rights that are not symmetrical. While the Ninth Amendment does recognize that the people possess more rights than are enumerated, there is not an inkling in the Declaration of Independence, the Constitution or the Bill of rights that points to "rights" that are anything but Natural, Unalienable rights. The tactics of the anti-Constitutionalist can be easily defeated if the people understand the illegitimate ruse they are trying to perform.

The Tenth Amendment goes hand in hand with the Ninth Amendment, and I view it as the exclamation mark amendment. It says:

> *The powers not delegated to the United States by the Constitution, nor prohibited by it to the states, are reserved to the states respectively, or to the people.*[40]

I can almost hear the framers saying (in today's voice); 'OK, we've consented to the federal government obtaining some limited, logical authority, but we've ceded only 26 things for which they are responsible, period! Got it?' The Tenth Amendment is the final clarifying statement by the framers that the federal government is to be a limited one. When one gains an understanding of the unmistakably clear intent of how our government was meant to work the actions of the anti-Constitutionalist are exposed as truly despicable.

So that's the Bill of Rights. Simple. Logical. Consistent. Its principles are traceable to the Declaration of Independence, and it is abundantly clear that the Bill of Rights intends to preserve the rights of the people and the states and to be sure the central government knows its place.

Let's take a moment to sum up where we are up to this point and see the intent, consistency, and the logical flow of thought of the nation's founding.

The colonies are being abused by the crown, they are not allowed to govern themselves they are not asked to consent to their rulers and the very nature of the ruler, a king, does not recognize their most basic of unalienable rights, that all men are created equal. They throw off their ties to their government and make the world-changing statements that *all men are created equal* and that the only legitimate power of government comes from the *consent of the governed*. They fight and win a war. Now they are faced with establishing a new central government. They naturally then start the process of establishing the role of the central government with delegates selected by each of the states to attend a Constitutional convention in an attempt to gain the consent necessary for that central government to be legitimate. They developed a system with various, separated powers checking one another and with the states checking the central government. The powers to be ceded by the states to the central government are defined and made finite. The delegates to the Constitutional convention agree to the terms and send their document to the states for the state's consent and to give birth to a new government. The states are clearly and understandably wary that the new central government is too powerful, but, in the end, they do consent as long as the first Congress brings up a Bill of Rights to further clarify the rights of the people and the states. The concept of a Bill of Rights, as agreed to is brought up in the first Congress and adopted serving as an exclamation mark at the end of the Constitution that screams that this is a central government whose only legitimate powers are those limited ones that through this transparent process we have consented to.

CHAPTER 12:

THE ANTI-CONSTITUTIONALIST'S ATTEMPT AT CONTROLLING LANGUAGE

~~~~~~~~~~~~~~~~~~~~~~~~~~~~~~~~~~~~~

Before we move on to some of the other amendments I want to take a moment to eradicate two of the illegitimate, uneducated and misleading arguments that the anti-Constitutionalist uses against we patriots. Those citizens who site the Constitution and advocate for an originalist's perspective are often called (among other things) Fascists and "Right Wing Nuts." First, let's see what fascism is with a brief (very) history lesson and learn about its beliefs, and maybe we'll discover who actually is a fascist in the process.

The etymology of the word Fascism shows us that it is rooted in a Roman word that literally means a bundle of rods, a suggestion of strength through unity. Fascism can trace its roots to the political unrest in Italy during and in the years immediately following the First World War. Benito Mussolini convened the first meeting of the Fascist party in March of 1915. In 1919 the Fascist Manifesto is published it advocated for totalitarian central government control over items such as, but not limited to: Education, Industry, labor, including trade unions, a minimum wage, public health, transportation, and communications. The Fascists abolished the Italian Senate, and they instituted increasingly progressive tax schemes. Fascism is a totalitarian form of government, Benito Mussolini, for all intents and purposes the founder of fascism described fascism this way:

> *Everything in the State, nothing outside the State, nothing against the State."[1]*

Now, what do God-given unalienable rights and limited, consented to government have to do with any of that? Let me see, who advocates for all that is fascism? Oh yeah, the anti-Constitutionalist does. It is the anti-Constitutionalist who desires absolute control over education, healthcare, commerce, etc. none of which are enumerated powers of the federal government. Those interested in the cause of liberty cannot let our adversaries define us, we cannot let them control the language. The deceit of the anti-Constitutionalist knows no bounds, in their minds, the end justifies the means. It is clear that someone who embraces our founding principles is about as far away from fascism as could possibly be, and the policies and tactics of the anti-Constitutionalist are precisely fascistic. When we look at the "mainstream" media and academia, we see an almost total control of messaging and no alternative thought will be tolerated, just as in Mussolini's Italy. Next time someone calls a Constitutionalist a fascist remember how Mussolini himself described fascism and think about that juxtaposed with the founding of our republic.

The anti-constitutionalist also tries to define Constitutional originalists as "Right Wing Nuts." What does "right-wing" mean and where does it come from and am I a "right-winger"? The term right-wing originates in France at the time of the French Revolution. The right-wing sat on the right side of parliament and were advocates for the monarchy of King Louis XVI. Hmmm, how can I be a right-winger if right-wingers support the Divine right of kings, I thought I believed that *all men are created equal*. Again the anti-Constitution-alist is merely trying to label the patriotic originalist in an undesir-able fashion. Isn't it the anti-Constitutionalists that get consumed with all things "royal" every time there is a wedding or a parade in London? It certainly isn't me.

If I'm not a right-winger, perhaps I am a left-winger. Let's see what that is. The left-wing which sat on the left side of the French par-liament (go figure) were advocates for what became the French Revolution and the dethroning of King Louis XVI. Out of the French Revolution, we get the Rights of Man, which was drafted in part by our very own Thomas Jefferson. As a very brief aside, I find the differences between the American and French Revolutions fascinating. And while it is a subject unto itself, I process the dis-tinction simply being the difference between an 'e' and an 'a.' The French Revolution was about that the Rights of Man, the American Revolution was about the Rights of Men. The difference being that the Rights of Man are collective rights and the Rights of Men are individual rights. So, since I am neither pro-monarch nor for col-lectives, I don't think I am either a left-winger or a right-winger. Over time, the notion of right-wing and left-wing evolved and the right-wing became associated with nationalistic and fascistic gov-ernments, which we know the Constitutional originalist is not and the left-wing became associated with Marxist governments, which we also know the Constitutional originalist is not either. So if the Constitutional originalist is neither right-wing nor left-wing how then does the political spectrum work?

I think the entire concept of right-wing and left-wing existing at opposite ends of a line is wrong. I don't think the political spectrum is a line at all. I think it is a circle. Think of it this way, were two of history's biggest villains really at the opposite end of the political spectrum? Adolf Hitler was supposedly right-wing, and Joseph Stalin was supposedly left-wing. Both were totalitarian, genocidal psychopaths, how is that opposite? Furthermore, I don't think that those who suffered under their rule would care about the esoteric difference in their economic policies. No, In fact, right-wing totalitarians are no different than left-wing totalitarians, they exist right next to each other on the political sphere. 180 degrees away from them is where the Constitutional originalist exists with his beliefs of God-given Unalienable rights and limited, consented to government.

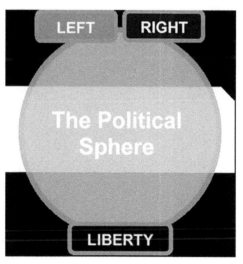

Next time you are accused of being a fascist or a right-winger explain this to your accuser, but stand back, their head is likely to explode.

We'll Move on now to the Eleventh and Twelfth Amendments. The Eleventh Amendment is ratified in 1795 and seeks to clarify the sovereign immunity of states. What I think is at least as important as the issue that the Eleventh Amendment deals with is the fact that the response of Congress to the issue was not to ignore or nullify the Constitution to obtain the result desired. Their natural response was to turn to Article Five and propose language to the states to gain their consent to change the way our government would work.

The Twelfth Amendment deals with the procedures for the election of the President and the Vice President. It was ratified in 1804, and it is the last of the amendments that are put forth by the founder's generation. The original Constitution had the runner-up of the Presidential election become the Vice President, I think we can all see through today's lens that Hillary would make a poor partner for President Trump. Rather than ignoring or "interpreting" the problem away, their natural response was proposing a solution to the states, asking for their consent to change our government. Ah, the good old days.

CHAPTER 13:

THE RECONSTRUCTION AMENDMENTS

~~~~~~

The next three amendments are collectively known as the reconstruction amendments. The Thirteenth Amendment freed the slaves. It says:

> *Neither slavery nor involuntary servitude, except as a punishment for crime whereof the party shall have been duly convicted, shall exist within the United States, or any place subject to their jurisdiction.*[1]

The tolerance of slavery within the states at the nation's founding was great hypocrisy and is certainly inconsistent with *all men are created equal*. I think it is essential to think about the Thirteenth Amendment in the light of the discussion we had about the way that the government grabs power today by solely focusing on whether or not a particular issue is a good idea or a bad idea and ignoring the issue of standing. No idea has ever been worse than slavery, yet the process by which slavery was dealt with was by the government first obtaining standing.

The stage is set for the Thirteenth Amendment by Abraham Lincoln's Emancipation Proclamation. Lincoln was an abolitionist, but the Emancipation Proclamation also had pragmatic and strategic benefits for the cause of the Union. Lincoln strategized that by freeing the slaves, he could hasten the defeat of the Confederacy in a couple of ways. Many slaves had been pressed into service for the Confederacy that, if freed would flee north, depriving the Confederacy of their service and cause chaos in the lines. Lincoln also needed to block possible European involvement in the war, as there was interest from the English and French in supporting the Confederacy. Lincoln knew that neither the English nor French would want to be seen as fighting for slavery alongside the Confederates. Lincoln needed to issue the proclamation after a Union victory on the battlefield to demonstrate the Union's ability to enforce the Proclamation, so shortly after the Union Victory (sort of) at Antietam (Sharpsburg), Maryland the Emancipation Proclamation was issued on September 22, 1862.

As momentous as the Proclamation was, it had little actual teeth to it. Abraham Lincoln was an originalist. He knew that his office only had the authority to faithfully execute the law. Lincoln knew that the federal government had no standing on the issue of slavery. So not only could Lincoln do nothing about slavery, neither could Congress (short of an amendment to the Constitution). So Lincoln's Emancipation Proclamation was issued only to those states in rebellion, who clearly wouldn't recognize Lincoln's authority. The slave states that remained loyal to the Union, Maryland, Delaware, Kentucky, and Missouri were unaffected by the proclamation.

Lincoln's Emancipation Proclamation went into effect on January 1st, 1863, and two years later, on January 31st, 1865, Congress proposes the Thirteenth Amendment. It is ratified that same year by the states, including those in the reconstructed south, on December 6, 1865. Several misconceptions regarding slavery and the Constitution exist. The Thirteenth Amendment is the first time that we see the word slavery in the Constitution. The word person (as in person held in service) was used as a means not to enshrine slavery at the federal level and to recognize the ultimate humanity of those held to service. Slavery was not enshrined in the Constitution, slavery was established at the state level. Arguments suggesting that the famous "three fifths clause" purpose was to reduce the value a slave to that of 60 percent of a white person are terribly misleading, and while the clause is in the document (Article One Section Two) the purpose of the three fifths clause was in fact to limit the proportional voting power of the slaveholding states in Congress. If the Constitution were a racist document, then all black men would have been subjected to the three-fifths rule; however free black men were counted the same as whites and blacks voted in as many as ten states prior to the civil war. Dismissing the Constitution as racist is just one more method that the anti-Constitutionalist uses to attempt to nullify the Constitution, the Constitution mentions neither slavery nor race. To see a racist Constitution, read the Constitution of the Confederacy.

The Thirteenth Amendment is also the first time that the federal government claims direct jurisdiction over the actions of individuals as no limit is placed on who it is that is holding another in bondage be they a state or an individual. The structure of the Thirteenth Amendment is also consistent with the original document; specifically, Article One Section Eight (the things Congress can do) where the overarching powers are laid out and then permission is granted to make laws pertaining to those powers through the necessary and proper clause. As such, the Thirteenth Amendment has its own necessary and proper clause. It says:

Congress shall have the power to enforce this article by appropriate legislation[2]

Because the power over slavery was not claimed by the central government under the initial Constitution, and therefore not subject to the *necessary and proper clause* (because that clause references *the foregoing powers*) Congress needed to explicitly granted the authority to take power away from the states to make laws to enforce the Thirteenth Amendment. So, even with something as obviously necessary as freeing the slaves, Congress knows its limitations and obtains consent from the states for the federal government to gain jurisdiction over the issue and the power to make necessary laws pertaining to it.

This is the true greatness of our Constitution. When society wishes to cure its ills, great and small, a process respectful of our founding principles is in place to gain consent from the governed to continue to make a more perfect union. It is in this sense that the Constitution should be embraced to unite us as a people and not distort the Constitution to divide us.

Today we increasingly hear about reparations being necessary to atone for the country's sin of slavery. This is an ugly business, not only is there no standing whatsoever for reparations to be made, who would be the recipient of the reparations and who would pay? Moreover, the central government never overtly condoned slavery (although it certainly recognized its existence in the states) slavery was implemented within the states so the states would have to pay? Which states? Since slavery officially ended with the ratification of the thirteenth amendment (remember, Lincoln could only free the slaves of the states in rebellion through the Emancipation Proclamation as he realized he had no standing within the states remaining in the Union), I am certain that there is neither slave nor slaveholder still living among us. And what of those who fought and died to liberate the slaves? Do they have to pay too? I know those from my heritage (northern Irish Catholic) fought against slavery, so I'm not paying. Will the country have to run DNA on its citizens to see who has to pay? Remember, the government has no money, never has, never will, the only money it has was taken, either legitimately or illegitimately (without consent) from the people. No, we constitutionalists understand our society is based on individual liberty, not some supposed "rights" based upon your allegedly aggrieved class.

The Fourteenth Amendment to the Constitution addresses a couple of issues, citizenship, and what I view as a reaffirmation of the Union after the rebellion. After the passage of the Thirteenth Amendment in 1865 Congress proceeded to pass the Civil Rights Act of 1866 (overriding a veto by President Johnson) which made assumptions based on freeing of slaves that they would necessarily have more rights bestowed upon them. Many thought this to be an unconstitutional overreach. So, as we have seen, as opposed to interpreting the problem away we see Congress affirmatively asking the states for the authority to change our government. Congress proposes the Fourteenth Amendment to the states in June of 1866, and it is ratified after extremely contentious debate in July of 1868. The time of reconstruction after the civil war was, to say the least, a difficult one for the country, yet it was critical that we remained faithful to the principles and processes of our republican form of government or we could never have won the peace.

The Fourteenth Amendment has five sections, four operative sections, and its own necessary and proper clause. The clause in the first section dealing with citizenship states:

All persons born or naturalized in the United States, and sub-ject to the jurisdiction thereof, are citizens of the United States and of the State wherein they reside.[3]

The issue of incorporation of former slaves into society began with the Thirteenth Amendment, which freed them. The Fourteenth Amendment now grants them citizenship. A clear, thorough, and originalist reading of the Fourteenth Amendment is critical. The Fourteenth Amendment does not bestow birthright citizenship. That would violate our two primary founding principles contained in the Declaration of Independence, *consent of the governed* and *all men are created equal*. Really, how so? First of all, birthright citizenship is a feudal notion, and it wasn't a right at all, it was an obligation. It obliged you to be the subject to a lord or prince or king, forever. You had no opportunity to consent to this condition and no way to escape this condition. Furthermore, the fact that birthright citizenship made you a subject to a royal flies directly in the face of *all men are created equal*.

The purposeful inclusion of *'subject to the jurisdiction thereof'* exists because to be a citizen of the United States an individual could not owe any other allegiances as in the example of both Indian tribes and foreign diplomats. Additionally, society needed to consent to your joining should you want to throw off those previous allegiances. To evidence this, starting in 1870 Congress begins inviting Indian tribes, in whole or in part to join the Union. Neither the tribes nor their members could simply self-declare themselves, citizens, just as today we citizens need to consent through an affirmative process to transfer the jurisdiction to which an alien is subject.

This clause of the Fourteenth Amendment also gives citizenship in the United States primacy over citizenship in the states which was desired after, in response to the Civil Rights Act of 1866, several states instituted "Black Codes" as an attempt to limit the rights of the freed slaves.

The next clause of the Fourteenth Amendment is known as the Equal Protection clause, it states:

> *No State shall make or enforce any law which shall abridge the privileges or immunities of citizens of the United States; nor shall any State deprive any person of life, liberty, or property, without due process of law; nor deny to any person within its jurisdiction the equal protection of the laws.*[4]

As always, we need to understand what the framers of the text were trying to solve for. They were simply trying to clarify that recently freed slaves had full citizenship rights. The requirement for the Fourteenth Amendment originates with the lack of specificity in the Thirteenth Amendment pertaining to the citizenship status of the newly freed slaves. This lack of specificity led to the Civil Rights Act of 1866, which was viewed as a potential overreach by the federal government, that overreach was countered by the "Black Codes," and the Fourteenth amendment attempts to clear up the whole issue. The first clause recognizes slaves now as citizens, and this next clause puts a fine clarifying point on the rights of these new citizens. It has three components. States could not deny citizens privileges, states could not selectively enforce laws, and all citizens had the same rights in front of the court.

We see the anti-Constitutionalist try to change the meaning of the word equal, but we know that the founders and framers meant equal under the law, not equal outcomes as they try to twist and reinterpret it into.

Section Two of the Fourteenth Amendment is an attempt to secure the right to vote for the freed slaves. Determining voter eligibility was left to the states, however, after the passage of the Thirteenth Amendment the three/fifths clause is effectively repealed resulting in an increase in the proportional representation in the Congress of the former slaveholding states. Section Two falls short of its goal, which is eventually accomplished via the Fifteenth Amendment. It is important here to realize that the states most likely would not have consented to the direct language of conferring voting rights on the freed slaves, but our process was followed, and while largely ineffectual it got closer to the goal without destroying the system in the process.

Sections Three and Four of the Fourteenth Amendment deal with issues arising from the rebellion. Section Three prohibits certain participants in the rebellion from holding office. Interestingly from a structural perspective, Section Three grants the power to Congress to override this provision with a two/thirds vote without any ratification from the states. Section Four Deals with Debt incurred during the rebellion, the Union debt stands, and the Confederate debt does not.

Section Five of the Fourteenth Amendment is its *necessary and proper* clause, again pointing to the finite, limited, and consented to nature of our government.

The Fifteenth Amendment to the Constitution is the third and last of the reconstruction era amendments it is designed to remedy the shortcomings in the Fourteenth Amendment Section Two, pertaining to voting rights for black Americans, freed slaves or otherwise. The Amendment is approved by Congress in February of 1869 and sent to the states for ratification. It is ratified in March of

1870. The Fifteenth Amendment is brief, with just two sections, one operative and the other its own necessary and proper clause, it reads:

> *The right of citizens of the United States to vote shall not be denied or abridged by the United States or by any State on account of race, color, or previous condition of servitude.*[5]

The Fifteenth Amendment is not perfect, no form of governance is. For the malevolent, there are always ways to circumvent clear intent. Practices such as requiring certain educational or property requirements were instituted to limit the effect on the amendment, poll taxes were instituted, but the governmental structure was made more sound and would, over time, cure the ill it was designed to cure.

I think the reconstruction era amendments were astounding. We emerge from a terrible civil war, somewhere on order of six to seven hundred thousand Americans perished during the conflict, but our republic survives. I process the reconstruction amendments this way (I know they do more). There is no complexity on the face of these amendments, only what some choose to see.

The Thirteenth Amendment frees the slaves

The Fourteenth Amendment makes them citizens

The Fifteenth Amendment gives them the right to vote.

Reconstruction is a brutal time in America's history, yet we endeavored to maintain the republic's founding principles, the states are asked to consent along the way as we made our union more perfect. There is no better idea than to ensure that all men are treated equally under the law, but how you achieve that matters because if you don't get the *consent of the governed* along the way you have defeated the entire purpose of our great American Experiment. A document that can cure mankind's ugliest sin must be a good document and to interpret it away is a sure way to lead us back to more of the evil of which mankind is capable.

CHAPTER 14:

THE PROGRESSIVE ERA AMENDMENTS

~~~~~~

The Sixteenth Amendment, income taxes. Yuck. The Sixteenth Amendment intends to achieve income taxes without apportionment among the states, or tax rates based on population, it reads:

The Congress shall have the power to lay and collect taxes on incomes, from whatever source derived, without apportionment among the several States, and without regard to any census or enumeration.[1]

During the early progressive era, the country begins its drift away from our founding principles, and many of the "elite" in the country are becoming smitten with European socialist ideas that are incompatible with our Constitutional republic. The federal government is hungry for income, and it becomes clear that to accomplish their goals, they are going to have to seek a Constitutional amendment to implement a non-apportioned income tax. This is obviously a contentious issue and some in Congress actually support the process of amendment because they believe it will be killed in the state ratifying conventions thereby ridding them of the issue for years to come. In July 1909 the proposed amendment was sent to the states for ratification. It is ratified in February of 1913.

I hate taxes. You likely hate taxes. While I certainly don't want to pay income tax, I do not believe the Sixteenth Amendment (by the way, I remember that the Sixteenth Amendment deals with taxes because both the word sixteen and tax each contain an x) is the actual problem. The problem instead lies in the way the Sixteenth Amendment is implemented. The central government asked the states to consent to a federal income tax, and they did. They played by the rules (I can't believe I am writing this). The problem I have from an originalist perspective is that while they played by the rules to attain the right to tax my income, they violated our other founding principle of *all men are created equal* in the implementation. Where does the federal government claim the right to look at two men, equal under God and the law and say one man pays a tax and another man is not only exempt but in fact, he takes the labor from his equal.

The Sixteenth Amendment's implementation is problematic because of who is taxed and not taxed, and because of what the federal government then spends the fruits of my labor on. It is here that the federal government has refused to ask for and receive my consent. Program after program after program that is not rooted in the 26 original items for which the federal government asked for and received consent take up a vast amount of the government's spending of my labor.

The ability to tax, income or otherwise, can only legitimately be viewed through the same lens as Article One, Section Eight's "necessary and proper" clause as the original power to tax is, in fact, one of the "foregoing powers." If Congress can only make laws that are necessary and proper to execute the foregoing twenty-six delineated items on Article One Section Eight of the Constitution, then they certainly can only use tax dollars (whatever the source) on those same items and no other. The breakdown in this relationship between the government and the people that began with FDR's "New Deal" programs when the Supreme Court surreptitiously recommended to the administration that because the federal government could tax that any program (law) cloaked in a tax would be viewed as legitimate by *that* Court. The same argument was used by the Court for the Affordable Care Act (AKA Obamacare). 1+1 does not equal three. The government does not have consent to tax for whatever purpose it deems fit, activist judges, who can only be and necessarily are anti-constitutionalists have, without consent, illegally taken power from the governed.

The Seventeenth Amendment to the Constitution is the second of the progressive era amendments. It takes the nation a step closer to a national government and a step away from our original federal government. The Seventeenth Amendment changes the method by which senators enter the Senate. Originally senators were appointed by the state legislatures, and the Seventeenth Amendment calls for senators to be elected by popular vote within their state. The Seventeenth Amendment passes Congress in May of 1912 and goes to the states for ratification. It is ratified a year later in May of 1913. The rationale for the necessity of the Seventeenth Amendment was a combination of a wave of populism sweeping the country and the perception that the Senatorial appointments led to corruption.

Whatever the rationale, after the ratification of the Seventeenth Amendment, the states have less of a direct check on the federal government. The framers believed in an active role for the states in the federal government. The notion of a senate with equal representation from the states, and whose members shall be appointed by the state legislatures was key to the Connecticut compromise that brought the large and small states together at the Philadelphia Convention. But again we see that the rules were followed and even though I personally do not like the outcome, I do honor the process. A Constitutional originalist would never be dismissive of a change to our government where the *consent of the governed* had been sought. I believe too much time is spent on the Seventeenth Amendment's change from state to direct elections as by the time of its passage a majority of states already had some form of direct election of senators. The more important issue is that senators and Congressmen alike are constantly operating outside of their clearly specified bounds and not asking for my consent.

We'll look at the Eighteenth and Twenty-First Amendments together. The Eighteenth Amendment prohibited the *manufacture, sale, or transportation of intoxicating liquors,* but not the consumption of intoxicating liquors. The Eighteenth Amendment passed Congress in December 1917 and was ratified by the states in January 1919. The amendment has several interesting attributes. It is the first time that an amendment grants concurrent enforcement with the states through the amendment's own "necessary and proper clause." Concurrent jurisdiction is a bit puzzling given the federal supremacy claimed in Article Six. It is also the first time we see a time limit by which the states would need to ratify the amendment after its passage in Congress (seven years).

The Eighteenth Amendment is another of the progressive era amendments, and unlike the prior two amendments, it clearly exhibits the progressive mentality of 'we know better than you do.' For a few decades prior to the passage of the Eighteenth Amendment, there was a growing temperance (no alcohol) movement in the country that was committed to eradicating the evils of alcohol and the damage the progressives believed alcohol was doing to society. The temperance movement, combined with the progressive's thinking that the government's role was to cure society's ills produced an ill-conceived, one-size-fits-all national solution to what was really a local problem.

We all know the stories and lore surrounding the ramifications of the ratification of the Eighteenth Amendment and its enabling legislation, the Volstead Act. The Country witnessed the rise of organized crime in America, people were being injured, or worse, from consuming poorly made "bathtub gin." The act proved unpopular and ineffective as the states were reluctant to enforce the act and juries were reluctant to convict those charged with violations of the act. Furthermore, many believed the act went beyond the amendment's intent by including beer and wine as well as liquor. These ramifications are the beginning of the many unintended consequences of an overreaching central government. The Eighteenth Amendment also heralds in the increased role of federal law enforcement. Under the original Constitution and the 26 items to which we consented there are only a couple that would require federal law enforcement, items such as the *Punishment of counterfeiting the Securities and current Coin of the United States.* Now, with a specific behavior being regulated at the federal level, we see the creation of the Prohibition Unit within the IRS (then called the Bureau of Internal Revenue). The Eighteenth Amendment, coupled with the federal government's access to more tax dollars provided by the Sixteenth Amendment led to the expansion of several federal law enforcement agencies, including entities within the Treasury and Justice Departments and the United States Coast Guard.

The Eighteenth Amendment is also the first time we see the government seek to control a specific behavior (liberty) of the people. Everything in the Constitution until the Eighteenth Amendment either describes how the government is to be formulated, limitations to be placed upon it or how the people's rights and liberties are to be protected.

I think the really interesting part of the Eighteenth Amendment is that it exposes today's anti-Constitutionalist progressive as a fraud. I think of the Eighteenth Amendment as the 'smoking gun' amendment. The progressive of 1917 is not yet the full anti-Constitutionalist we see today. The progressive of 1917 realized that restricting people's access to alcohol was well beyond the framer's conception of the limited role of the central government. He realizes that he has no standing in the issue of liquor unless the Constitution is amended.

Today's anti-Constitutionalist will tell you that the Constitution is outdated, yet just one hundred years ago the progressive uses the Constitution's processes to accomplish his goals. The progressive from one hundred years ago still seeks (whether he wants to or not) the *consent of the governed*. If the Constitution's notions were not outdated one hundred years ago for the early progressive, how can they be outdated today? Particularly when today's anti-Constitutionalist turns to a document that was written *one hundred fifty* years ago in the works of Marx. Furthermore, not only does the anti-Constitutionalist of today not use the Constitution's amendment process to gain *the consent of the governed*, he further circumvents the system as he ignores Article One Section One of the Constitution which says plainly that all laws come from Congress. It is much easier for the anti-Constitutionalist to achieve his goals, without your consent through the government's unelected, unaccountable bureaucracy.

The Twenty-First Amendment repeals the Eighteenth Amendment and effectively gives control of Alcohol regulation back the states (although the federal government continued the excise taxes imposed), several of which remained dry states for years to come. The Twenty-First Amendment is the only amendment that specifically wholly repeals another amendment. Other amendments do render particular sections of other amendments moot, but only this amendment repeals another amendment explicitly. Congress passed The Twenty-First Amendment in February 1933, and it is ratified by the state conventions (state ratifying conventions were a requirement of the amendment) in December of 1933.

Prohibition was the first large scale effort by the federal government to encroach on the individual liberties of citizens. The required Constitutional amendment process was followed; however, the spirit of the founding of the country was dead. When prohibition is repealed in 1933 during Franklin Roosevelt's first presidential term, the nation will never again adhere to the notion of limited consented to government and that *all men are created equal*. The Country enters into an era where one man can bestow "rights" upon another as the country rejects the universal nature of unalienable god-given rights. From this point on all additional federal power-grabs will be done without the consent of the governed through Congress, the courts, and bureaucrats.

The Nineteenth Amendment to the Constitution prohibits states from determining voter qualification based on sex. Its operative text reads:

The right of citizens of the United States to vote shall not be denied or abridged by the United States or by any State on account of sex.[2]

Congress passed the Nineteenth Amendment in June of 1919, and the states ratify it in August of 1920. The Nineteenth Amendment is the last of the "progressive era" amendments. Following its operative clause, the Nineteenth Amendment also has its own necessary and "proper clause" as we continue to see the consistent methodology whereby as Congress obtains consent to gain purview over an issue, they then need the authority to legislate around their new authority. This consistent methodology of amendments inclusive of their own necessary and proper clause is among the strongest arguments for the original intent of the necessary and proper clause found at the end of Article One, Section Eight.

It is often miscommunicated that the original Constitution prohibited women from voting. It did no such thing. The anti-Constitutionalist uses that argument to intentionally mislead people to believe that the founders were anti-woman. If we go back to founding principles, we can easily disprove this notion. First of all, the founders certainly believed women are included in the concept of *all men are created equal*. Secondly, and more importantly the central government was meant to be a limited one, there were only 26 items to which the states ceded control and determining who could vote and who could not vote was not one of those claimed central powers. Determining who could vote was left to the states explicitly. Immediately following Article One, Section One, which says all laws come out of Congress, Article One Section Two leaves to the states who may vote. So, the Constitution does not prohibit women from voting. Instead, the Constitution demonstrates the intended limited role for the central government by reserving voting rights to the states.

The Constitution, through its Amendment process allows for any manner of change to which the people wish to consent. Be it a grave and important idea such as prohibiting holding a fellow man in bondage or a small and comparatively unimportant idea such as prohibiting access to alcohol. So too with the right to vote, whether that is the freed slaves via the Fifteenth Amendment or women here in the Nineteenth Amendment, the framework provided for in Article Five exists for society to shape itself as it sees fit through gaining the consent of the governed.

CHAPTER 15:

MORE STRUCTURAL AMENDMENTS

~~~~~~~~~~~~~~~~~~~~~~~~~~~~~~

The Twentieth Amendment was proposed to address two structural issues in the original Constitution; lame-duck terms and presidential succession. The time between an election and the new government taking its seat is called a lame-duck session. Congress passes the Twentieth Amendment in March of 1932, and it is ratified in January of 1933. At the time, it is the fastest ratification of any amendment. The Twentieth Amendment has six sections, four operative sections, two dealing with lame-duck sessions and two dealing with presidential succession the final two sections are administrative.

In September of 1788, at the time of the ratification of the original Constitution the Confederation Congress chooses March 4, 1789, for the new government to commence. In 1845 the first Tuesday in November became Election Day making the time from election to enactment about one hundred and twenty days. Lame-duck sessions are not desirous because politicians who have not been re-elected have diminished influence as they will not be carrying on in the next session and at the same time they can advance policy or legislation that may be in conflict with his newly-elected replacement.

The original Constitution leaves to the state legislatures the *Times, Places and Manner* for electing senators and representatives. Congress is required to meet once a year, at the beginning of December. The Twentieth Amendment reduces the impact of lame-duck sessions by changing the commencement of the term of the presidency from March 4 to January 20, and Congress' term is to commence on January 3. The Twentieth Amendment also changes the date of the required yearly meeting of Congress from the first Monday in December to January 3. Lame-duck sessions still exist; however, their impact is reduced from roughly one hundred twenty days to seventy-five days.

The other two operative sections of the Twentieth Amendment deal with the question of presidential succession. The original Constitution does not address the issue of how a president will be selected should the newly elected president not be inaugurated. The issue that these sections of the Twentieth Amendment contemplate had never arisen, but the concern was that the country always needs a clear path to seating a president even in the unlikely scenarios that the amendment addresses.

The Administrative sections of the Twentieth Amendment state the date that, if ratified, the amendment becomes effective. And similar to the Eighteenth Amendment it places a seven-year time frame by which the states need to ratify.

Simple, logical, and consistent, the Twentieth amendment uses the process put in place by Article Five to address perceived structural issues in the Constitution. Whether or not the solutions were the ideal solutions is not the point of this book. The point is that desired change went through the established process, consent was sought and granted, and the machinery of our government is changed, and our Union is made just a little bit more perfect.

The Twenty-Second Amendment deals with the issue of presidential term limits. Article Two (which deals with the executive branch of government) of the Constitution places no limits on how many four year terms a president may serve so Congress, so, as opposed to implementing a change by statute, reaches out to the people to gain their consent to limit the term of the president. The Twenty-Second Amendment is passed by Congress in March of 1947 and is ratified by the states in February of 1951. The Twenty-Second Amendment limits the amount of time that an individual can serve as president to a maximum of ten years. An individual can be elected to two four year terms provided he has not served as president for more than two years of a term to which he was not elected. If he has served more than two years of a term to which he was not elected, then he is limited to a single additional term. The Twenty-Second Amendment also contains the expiration provision requiring the amendment's ratification by the states within seven years of its passage through Congress. The amendment is a direct reaction to the unprecedented four terms of Franklin Roosevelt.

Until Franklin Roosevelt, there had never been a president who served more than two terms; however, two presidents have been unsuccessful in their attempts to do so; Ulysses Grant and Theodore Roosevelt. Ulysses Grant attempted a run for a third term after a four-year break following his two terms in office; however, he did not gain his party's nomination for president. Theodore Roosevelt served the remaining three years of William McKinley's term after McKinley's assassination in 1901. Roosevelt was then elected president in his own right and served until 1909. Then following a four-year break after the end of his second term Roosevelt ran for the presidency again, but he was defeated by Woodrow Wilson.

The concept of term limits (what was called rotation at the time) has an interesting history, predating the Constitution. Under the Articles of Confederation, delegates were subject to a three-year term limit for any six years, and while there was no executive branch under the Articles, there was a, largely ceremonial, president of the Congress that served for one year. John Hanson of Maryland was elected to that office in November of 1781 making Hanson the first president of the United States (sort of). Hanson was not a great fan of the job and tried to resign, but the Articles contained no plan for succession. Succession is one of the many areas that we see addressed in the Constitution in our attempt to make a more perfect Union.

The concept of term limits was discussed at the Constitutional Convention, and there were differing views. James Madison was against term limits for Congress as he believed the constant rotation would lead to dysfunction (well Madison got almost everything else right). Madison also did not want to deprive the best people for the job the opportunity to serve. He had, obviously not met our current merry band of nitwits and fools serving in Congress. Hamilton too was against term limits as he was an advocate for a strong presidency. Jefferson, on the other hand, who was not at the Convention was against presidential term limits saying:

> *"The...feature I dislike, and greatly dislike, is the abandonment in every instance of the necessity of rotation in office, and most particularly in the case of the President,"*[1]

Our tradition of presidents serving two terms is the result of the precedent set by George Washington. Washington's refusal to seek a third term is perhaps his greatest and most patriotic act as men do not often relinquish power once it is granted to them. With typical Washington humility, the manner in which he declines to run for a third term is very matter-of-fact. Washington even tells the American people in his Farewell Address that he believes he was never qualified to be president in the first place. The tradition of a maximum two-term presidency lasts until 1940 when Franklin Roosevelt break with tradition when he is elected to a third term and in 1944 to a fourth.

It was during Roosevelt's tenure that the government goes completely off the rails. Roosevelt's first term commences during the deepest part of the great depression, and Roosevelt uses the crisis to massively expand central government power by implementing his New Deal without going through the legitimizing step of asking for consent through the amendment process. Many today are told to believe that the New Deal helped the U.S. emerge from the Great Depression. I don't want to look at whether or not it was a good idea (which I certainly don't think it was) I want to look at it from a standing and process and power grab perspective. Let's look at the programs of the First New Deal which began during the first one hundred days of Roosevelt's first term and see if they are rooted in consented to powers granted to the central government either in the original Constitution or through amendment.

The Emergency Banking Relief Act was enacted to assist private banks which were struggling and failing during the great depression. Article One, Section Eight of the Constitution gives Congress the authority to coin money and regulate its value, it says nothing about propping up failing private businesses.

The Civilian Conservation Corps was established to provide government jobs to unmarried young men, to among other things, plant trees. A quick read of Article One, Section Eight will show you that it does not mention trees.

The Agricultural Adjustment Act was established to raise agricultural prices that were falling because of increased efficiencies, God forbid. The Act paid farmers to destroy and or not produce agricultural goods. Article One Section, Eight of the Constitution does not mention agriculture in any way, the only mention of commerce at all is Congress' power to regulate commerce *among* the several states.

The Federal Emergency Relief Act was a federal grant program to provide state and local government jobs in an attempt to reduce unemployment. Article One, Section Eight of the Constitution does not grant the central government the power to fund state and local government programs.

The Tennessee Valley Authority was established to, among other things, run power plants and make fertilizer in the southeastern United States. Article One, Section Eight of the Constitution does not mention power plants. But how could it, there were no power plants in 1788? Technological advancement is not a legitimate reason for the central government to grab power.

The Federal Securities Act was instituted to regulate the sale of securities, essentially the stock market. Again Article One, Section Eight's Commerce Clause was to regulate interactions among the states, not the businesses within the states.

The Federal Deposit Insurance Corporation was instituted to ensure commercial bank deposits. Article One, Section Eight, does not mention providing insurance to patrons of private corporations.

The National Recovery Administration was designed to ensure fair competition and fair play among and between farmers, labor, and industry, including price and wage controls. Article One, Section Eight, does not give the central government any authority over farmers, labor, industry, wages, or prices.

The Public Works Administration was established to fund large infrastructure projects such as bridges, dams, and tunnels, including the Lincoln Tunnel. Article One, Section Eight, does not give the central government authority to engage in infrastructure projects.

The above list is meant to be illustrative, not exhaustive. Contained within these various acts and programs are other bureaucratic creations that played a role in the implementation of the New deal. These New Deal programs started in 1933. So all of this government overreach takes place just fourteen years after the passage of the Eighteenth Amendment (prohibition). What has changed in those fourteen short years? Less than two decades prior, in 1919, Congress knew it did not have the standing to regulate alcohol, so they sought the power to do so by proposing an amendment to the Constitution. Now in 1933, Congress claims control of society through statute. What changed was the great depression. Bad times for the people are a good time for despots. The benefits that the despot is claiming are always 'for the good of the people.' Dictatorships are not born in good times.

The arguments for these types of programs are always of the sort that it is a 'good idea.' Standing is never part of the anti-constitutionalists playbook.

I imagine that some reading this will be put off by my calling Franklin Roosevelt a despot, but he was, sorry. Let's see what happens after the first new deal goes into effect. Several provisions of the New Deal were struck down as being unconstitutional (I promised I wouldn't go into Constitutional law so you can research which ones privately). To me, which provisions were struck down is not nearly as interesting as to how Roosevelt reacted. In 1937 after suffering the court defeats surrounding some of his New Deal programs, Roosevelt advocated for the Judicial Procedures Reform Bill. The Bill sought to expand the number of Supreme Court Justices so that Roosevelt can appoint justices that would be sympathetic to his new deal programs. Roosevelt sought to stack the court. Tell me that isn't the action of a despot. Despots don't just strut around in military uniforms, sometimes they speak grandfatherly to you while wearing a sweater and sitting in front of the fire.

Roosevelt's Second New Deal Goes into effect beginning in 1935, and it is here we find the advent of our current social security system. Exactly how a legitimate argument can be made for a government insurance program for individuals is confounding. Every single thing we see that the framers of the Constitution put in place as it pertains to individuals is about the central government simply ensuring an individual's right to pursue happiness by both limiting the government's role in society and by recognizing the God-given, unalienable rights of the individual. Now with Roosevelt, we see the primary theme of the central government evolve into simply a wealth redistribution apparatus. Roosevelt and his cronies never ask for society's consent; they use a crisis (the Great Depression) to seize power. The fact is, the anti-constitutionalists just wanted the programs that they wanted, so they twisted reality into a pretzel and *voila*. As I said early on, everyone is biased, Supreme Court Justices included. We need to understand those biases and only choose those who will be faithful to the rule of law, not those anti-constitutionalists who will enshrine their policies using and illegitimate cloak of legitimacy.

I think by now we can see all of these programs fly directly in the face of the limited, enumerated and consented to government that the framers of the constitution established.

Anyway, I find it somewhat amusing after all of this overreach that the Twenty-Second Amendment is ratified to reduce the likelihood of another long term presidential despot.

The Twenty Third Amendment to the Constitution addresses the issue of the citizens of the District of Columbia voting in presidential elections. Congress passes the amendment in June of 1960, and it is ratified by the states in March of 1961.

Article One, Section Eight of the Constitution establishes the notion of a district, separate and apart from any state as the seat of the central government. This logical idea prevented any state from gaining an advantage (or disadvantage) of also serving as the seat of the central government. We see the continued recognition of the intended limited nature of the central government as this district is limited to no more than 100 square miles. Since Washington D.C. became the seat of government in the United States in 1790, its residents could vote for neither the president nor members of Congress. The Twenty Third Amendment limits the electors of the District of

Columbia to be no more than those attributed to the smallest state, irrespective of the actual population in the District.

The Twenty Third Amendment does not give the citizens of the District the ability to vote for members of Congress. The perceived (or real) injustice is sufficiently irritating to the citizens of the District that they have adopted the slogan *Taxation without representation* for their motor vehicle license plates.

The Twenty Third Amendment solves a simple, structural problem. I think that the important takeaway is that Congress goes through the trouble of using the amendment process to address this simple issue, they don't just legislate the problem away. Why Congress, at that time chooses to deal with the issue through the amendment process is unclear, but what we are now seeing is a central government dealing with issues large and small in an increasingly arbitrary way. Just twenty-seven years earlier in 1933, the government changes its nature and relationship with the states and individuals by statute, and that those changes are illegitimately made legitimate by an out of control court. No longer do we live in a Constitutional Republic, and we have lost it because the central government never asked for its powers to become universal.

Lastly, the Twenty Third Amendment again contains its own *Necessary and Proper* Clause. The continued and consistent use of individual *Necessary and Proper* clauses within individual amendments as the government asks for more power makes it absolutely clear of the intent of the original *Necessary and Proper* Clause in Article One, Section Eight. The purpose and structure and the use of these clauses are identical; new power is granted to the central government, and they now need to gain specific permission to legislate around that power because these new powers are not included in the original *foregoing powers.*

The Twenty Fourth Amendment prohibits the use of poll taxes in federal elections by both the central government and by the states. The Twenty Fourth Amendment passed Congress in August 1962, and it was ratified by the states in January 1964. The language of the Twenty Fourth Amendment was careful to limit the prohibition to federal elections as there was a concern by the framers of the amendment of the central government further encroaching into state elections.

The Twenty Fourth Amendment also contains its own *necessary and proper* clause as it is the only way Congress could legislate around the issue because this issue was not considered in either the Constitution's original 26 items over which the central government gained purview or any of the twenty-three preceding amendments. Are you seeing a pattern yet?

The necessity for the Twenty Fourth Amendment stems from the intentional disenfranchisement of blacks and poor white voters after the ratification of the Fifteenth Amendment. Several southern states, including all from the former Confederacy engaged in implementing poll taxes in various ways. Those states chose poll taxes as their method of discrimination because the language of the Fifteenth Amendment expressly prohibited restricting an individual's right to vote based on race, so because most blacks in the south were poor, the poll tax was particularly impactful on them. The southern states that engaged in poll taxes knew the Fifteenth Amendment intended to allow blacks to vote, but similar to how Congress ignored Constitutional limitations placed on them so did these southern states as they attempted to nullify the Constitution by state statutes.

The Twenty Fourth Amendment again proves that the Constitution is far from the racist, misogynist document claimed by the anti-constitutionalist. It is, in fact, the Constitution that cures the ills that it is claimed to cause: Through the Thirteenth Amendment, the Constitution ends slavery. Through the Fifteenth Amendment, the Constitution recognizes the rights of blacks to vote. Through the Nineteenth Amendment, the Constitution recognizes a woman's right to vote. And now, here with the Twenty Fourth Amendment, it is the Constitutional process that closes a loophole used by several states to avoid the intent of the Fifteenth Amendment.

In the original Constitution, there was a lot of deference paid to the states when it came to elections eligibility and requirements. As time went on, it became clear to society the central government should become more involved in setting those election requirements. Congress used the amendment process to request and gain consent from the states to establish more uniform election rules. How is the Constitution, when applied, not a document for good?

The Twenty-Fifth Amendment again deals with presidential succession. The amendment is passed by Congress in July of 1965 and is ratified by the states In February 1967. The Twenty-Fifth Amendment attempts to remove any ambiguities regarding presidential and vice-presidential succession that exist in Article Two. Since the Constitution's ratification, there have been several presidents who die or become incapacitated while in office and Congress sought a means to remedy the lack of clarity around the issue permanently. While several interesting instances evidence the legitimate reasons that Congress sought a long term solution for presidential succession that is not really the purpose of this book. Recently, however, anti-constitutionalists have sought to use Twenty-Fifth Amendment authority to unseat a legitimately elected president for strictly political purposes. The anti-constitutionalist claims, and seeks like-minded "experts" to validate their claims that the president is somehow unstable and can no longer fulfill the duties of his office. This is, of course, ludicrous; they simply don't like him, his supporters or his policies. This type of disrespect for the Constitution and using it for their own political desires is both despicable and typical of the anti-constitutionalist. The anti-constitutionalist refuses to look at the legitimate purpose and intent of the amendment, clarity around succession, and instead politicizes it.

The structure and process of instituting the Twenty-Fifth Amendment is important, like all of the preceding amendments. The central government now asks the states for permission to change or expand upon an existing Constitutional concept to which the states have previously consented. If the central government seeks legitimate change to increase (or decrease) its authority, seek consent through the amendment process.

The Twenty-Sixth Amendment deals with voting age, lowering it from twenty-one to eighteen. The Twenty-Sixth Amendment is ratified is a shorter period of time than any other amendment. It passes Congress in March of 1971 and is ratified in July of 1971, a little over 3 months. Several previous legislative attempts had been made to lower the voting age, but it was determined that Congress had no such standing as the states controlled the terms of their elections. The increasingly unpopular war in Southeast Asia was seeing conscripted young men fighting and dying in Viet Nam who could not yet vote, Congress sought a change and the States consented, just the way it is supposed to happen. The Twenty-Sixth Amendment does further encroach on decisions that the states can make, but they consented to it, therefore legitimizing the taking of power. I have to wonder today if all of the "red" "flyover" states would cede such authority, whether the merits warrant it or not. The Twenty-Sixth Amendment also features its own 'necessary and proper clause' as Congress would have no authority to make additional laws regarding this issue if they had not been granted that authority by the states. I think it should now be unmistakably clear what the original intent of the Necessary and Proper clause was and is.

The Twenty Seventh, and last Amendment deals with Congressional compensation. While the Twenty-Sixth Amendment took the least amount of time to ratify, the Twenty Seventh took the most time. The Twenty Seventh Amendment was one of the original twelve amendments sent to the states for ratification in September 1789, it was ratified in May of 1992, more than 200 years after being proposed. This simple amendment states that Congress cannot have its compensation altered without an intervening election. The concern is obvious, they did not want Congress voting themselves pay increases without consequence for their actions, further evidencing the framer's distrust of government and seeking to further limit the power of the central government without consent from the governed.

So that is your Constitution. I don't see the alleged complexity alleged that has attempted to dissuade us from reading and understanding the Constitution. I didn't need to get into a time machine to understand it. Its origins in the Declaration of Independence are obvious. Its structure is plain and consistent. It is not allegorical it is meant to be read as it is written.

The United States of America is the only country in the history of mankind formed for the sole purpose to place the individual above the state and to limit the control that the government can have over its citizens. All other governments have been instituted to make citizens subjects by using the guise of "rights" that, in fact, create obligations, that are enforced with the barrel of a gun.

The Constitution is the framework that codifies the quintessentially American principles put forth in the Declaration of Independence. The Constitution is really just a legal 'mother may I?' asked of the states by the central government as well serving as the organizational rule book by which the central government is meant to operate for us to form a more perfect union. The Constitution is straight forward; it is clearly written, and it is finite.

CHAPTER 16:

COMMUNISM AND THE CONSTITUTION

~~~~~~~~~~~~~~~~~~~~~~~~~~~~~~~~~~~~

Communism is illegal in the United States. If the U.S. Constitution was faithfully applied, I believe the result would be liberty, not perfection, but liberty nonetheless. Instead, our heavy-handed central government of today looks much more like the Communism of Friedrich Engels and Karl Marx than it does the country that Madison and the other framers imagined. Communism, in all of its forms and off-shoots, including (but not limited to) socialism, progressivism, democratic socialism, national socialism, fascism is a totalitarian, fascistic (the state is everything) form of government where the state (read as the "elite" running the state) has absolute control over every aspect of its subjects lives. If American Constitutionalism is the closest thing to a governmental system that produces liberty, Communism, is the governmental system that will produce near-ubiquitous slavery. Communism is evil.

Moreover, in our Constitutional system, Communism is illegal. To be clear, when I say that communism is illegal, I don't mean that communists are illegal, I mean that their policies are illegal. To say that communists are illegal would be violative of the First

Amendment. The limits placed on the federal government by the states should have made Communism impossible to implement without amendments to the Constitution. However, every day we creep perilously closer to losing our Constitutional republic forever to the darkness of Communism (or any of the other Isms). My use of the term Communism is neither alarmism nor hyperbole. Today's "progressives" are flat of communists, they are just largely too cowardly, and or ignorant to admit it, instead using euphemisms such as "democratic socialists." As with the previous arguments that have been put forth in this book, I will not debate the merits of communism as there is no standing whatsoever for the kind of state power that communism requires in a Constitutional republic. In a Constitutional Republic founded on the *consent of the governed,* you must first attain my permission before you implement your "great idea." The anti-constitutionalists never so much as mentions how they can legitimately implement their system that will totally control your life. The media too is complicit in this scheme as they continue to bank on your ignorance to implement their plans.

Today we see near-constant coverage of the "progressive agenda" put forth by the democratic socialists. We see the fawning discussion of the merit of ludicrous ideas such as the "Green New Deal." Well, my fellow citizen, if we don't start insisting on having these "elites" tell us where exactly they get their Constitutional authority for such programs, we will be a full-blown socialist country in a decade or less from the time the anti-constitutionalists gain control of our three branches of government. At that point Liberty is dead and the Great American Experiment is over.

Let's look at some of the ideas and methods by which the anti-constitutionalist Marxist uses to advocate for communism, socialism, progressivism, although rarely presented as such. These will likely seem familiar as the playbook of the anti-constitutionalist is not particularly creative.

1. **American Constitutionalism is outdated thought:** Today's anti-constitutionalist communist always and without exception start their argument not on whether or not they have standing for their ideas but with flat out nullification, the Constitution is old and filled with outdated ideas. This practice is not only illegal (as the people have not supplanted the constitution with another form a government) but dangerous. If the anti-constitutionalists ideas are acceptable are anyone's? What if all unpopular speech was deemed illegal (something else to which we are creeping perilously close) by those in power? Can we outlaw private property by nullification? This is a dangerous slope that will only lead to anarchy, or worse.

   Central to the Constitution's construct is that it can, through the consent of the governed, be changed infinitely via Article Five. Any document that can be infinitely changed cannot be outdated. The Anti-constitutionalist communist will say that the document is over 200 years old, true. The Constitution was ratified in 1788, 231 years ago as of this writing. Engels and Marx wrote the Communist Manifesto in 1848, 171 years ago. So you're telling me that in the 60 years between the ratification of the Constitution and the publication of the Communist Manifesto the essence humanity dramatically changed. What makes 231-year-old thought outdated and 171-year-old thought modern? Men were still traveling on horseback, shooting single shot, smoothbore muskets, living with no central heat or cooling and existing with primitive health care yet those 60 intervening years magically create modern thought; I don't think so. In fact, totalitarians have wanted to forcibly coerce populaces into compliance for time immemorial. There are really only two schools of thought; people can live in liberty, or they can live under tyranny, there always have been those two schools of thought and always will be only those two schools of thought. It wasn't until the American Revolution and the implementation of limited constitutional government that liberty was the law of the land. No, American Constitutionalism is not outdated thought, tyranny through progressivism, communism, and socialism represent the archaic and repressive thought.

2. **Capitalism is Evil**: The framers never heard the term capitalism, a term coined by Marx and Engels. Instead, the framers and founders, many of whom were merchants of one sort or another instinctively knew about profit, it was the sole reason they traded in various goods. Within the Constitution, there is no concept whatsoever regarding restricting trade or how much profit could be earned. On the contrary Article One Section Eight's commerce clause was originally intended to ensure free trade among the states, enabling individuals in one state to sell, and yes, profit in another state. There is no standing for the government to limit one's profit. Profit is not bad, or as Gordon Gecko said, greed is good. The free market (I will not use the word capitalism as I will not be defined by Marx) is precisely the environment that the anti-constitutionalists hold in disdain. The free market is called free because individuals enter into voluntary transactions, and in a society based on the free market, those transactions are virtually infinite. In its free state, an economy is so complex that it makes attempts to regulate it to gain a particular outcome doomed

to failure. A free market drives competition to areas of high profit, driving down prices toward costs. I ask the anti-constitutionalist communist one question if there is no profit motive, please explain to me capital formation. Absent the profit motive none of these anti-constitutionalists could sip Starbucks coffee while looking at their iPhones and wearing their Birkenstocks. Irrespective of the logic of "capitalism" any state-controlled system is unconstitutional.

3. **The Possibility of Leisure:** One of the more inane arguments made in our post-constitutional world is that people should have the ability to pursue their "dreams." Certainly, everyone has the right to pursue their happiness, but what the anti-constitutional communist is referencing is that you should be able to pursue your leisure at the expense of someone else's labor to fund your life's necessities. Pursuing leisure is just one example of the type of "right" the anti-constitutionalist wants to grant to citizens that is actually an obligation, an obligation to give your labor to someone unwilling to work. The government clearly has no standing to take one person's property and give it to another so she can study rug hooking.

4. **Technological Advancement:** The anti-constitutionalist communist will often attempt to nullify the Constitution by stating that the world is far more technologically advanced today and that the founders and framers could never contemplate our "complex" world. I say rubbish on every front. The founders and framers never envisioned an iPhone but so what? How does technological advancement enable government usurpation of my God-given unalienable rights? Why, because the world has more gadgets does that mean

the government no longer needs my consent? It does not. With typical hypocrisy, those espousing this idea do not place the same standard on limiting the media's influence in the same drastically changed technologically advanced world. What the founders and framers did know is that the world *would* change and that the government should be able to evolve over time but that society would need to consent to those changes for the government to remain legitimate. The amendment process laid out in Article Five is the nemesis of the anti-constitutionalist who make these arguments; they hope you are unfamiliar with the process.

5. **The Idle Rich:** The anti-constitutionalist communist hold the rich in disdain, but none more than those who attain their wealth through inheritance. This disdain highlights their fundamental belief that the government owns everything, why should your progeny be granted wealth after your passing? The fact is that the government has no standing in your wealth, it is your God-given, unalienable right to do with it what you please. We now see an attempt at an across the board grab at wealth by communists who support a tax, not on your income, but on your wealth. Well, if the country needed to pass the Sixteenth Amendment to institute the income tax, isn't an amendment also needed to institute a wealth tax?

6. **Education**: The anti-constitutionalist claims to love education; in fact, the anti-constitutionalist love propaganda and indoctrination. As we have discussed, neither does the word education, nor the concept of education appear anywhere in the Constitution. As with many evil regimes throughout history, controlling the minds of the young is not only

desirable but critical. We see the anti-constitutionalist in lock-step with both the union-controlled public education system and the "elites" of our institutions of "higher education." Ask yourself this. Why do the taxpayers, through the federal government, fund colleges? There is clearly no standing. Why are the anti-constitutionalists advocating free college; why are they insistent that high school graduates go to college; Why do they want nationalized student debt and debt forgiveness?

7. **Attempting to establish special classes of citizens:** We increasingly see the intentional balkanization of the U.S. citizenry. No more do all individuals meld into society through a "melting pot." Today citizens are no longer looked at as individuals, instead the anti-constitutionalist lumps all of us into specific groups and ascribes either positive or negative, aggrieved and aggrievor status to these groups. The process of balkanization is foisted upon us by using the euphemistic term "diversity." In today's society, you cannot escape people claiming to be from some put-upon group. Why are these people claiming to be from a class of people as opposed to being individuals with a divine spark and God-given unalienable rights? The Constitution only calls for the betterment of the "General Welfare" (emphasis on General). In fact, the desire to not repeat the balkanization of Europe and its never-ending wars was one of the most potent reasons put forth by the framers when arguing for the necessity of a "More Perfect Union" and those arguments were articulated in the first dozen, or so, Federalist Papers. Until the last few decades, when the anti-constitutionalist began to put forth their Trojan horse of diversity, the country recognized the relationship between unity

and peace. The anti-constitutionalist cannot implement his schemes if we see ourselves as individuals, united with an understanding of our unalienable rights. The anti-constitutionalist needs to divide us into groups opposed to one another. In this scheme, instead of having unalienable rights, our "rights" would be forced upon us by someone who has no intention of asking for your consent as he does not see himself as your equal. The constant discord sewn by the anti-constitutionalist has become transparent, and we need to be vigilant in adhering to our individualism and steadfast in the understanding of our unalienable rights

8. **Law school:** I used to wonder how so many lawyers could be anti-constitutionalists, I don't anymore. In my research for writing this book, I read a "Constitutional Law" book. It was an eye-opener, to say the least. In this book on what they called "Constitutional Law," almost no time was spent on the context in which the Constitution was written. How can you tell young law students how the Constitution is to be applied when you don't tell them the tenets of Americanism of which the Constitution was meant to enshrine? With no explanation of the Declaration of Independence, one cannot possibly understand the Constitution. Additionally, there was no meaningful discussion of Article Five. Without a thorough examination of how 'we the people' can change the Constitution, one could be led to believe that it is incumbent upon the courts to evolve the Constitution's meaning over time. Moreover, there was substantial discussion meant to persuade the student away from originalism, and not a word attempting the counter-argument dismissing the illegal notion of the

elitist, anti-constitutional "living, breathing" Constitution. To call law school a sham is to defame shams.

9. **The pie is finite:** The anti-constitutionalist also espouses silly and uneducated (and dangerous) economic theories. These theories are rooted in emotions meant to divide our society. Today there is an extraordinary amount of time talking about the "wealth gap." The gap between rich and poor is no business of the government; there is nothing in the Constitution that bestows the authority upon the central government to redistribute wealth. Moreover, the rationale used by the anti-Constitutionalist presumes that wealth is finite. Wealth is, of course, not finite. The pie is not a fixed size. The fact that one becomes wealthy does not preclude another from becoming equally or more wealthy. The argument used by the anti-constitutionalist is pure emotion and simply attempts to pit Americans against one another and bring out the worst of human emotions at the same time absolving one for lack of productivity and persecuting another for too much productivity. How can it possibly matter to someone that Warren Buffet, for example, is a multi-billionaire? Buffet did not take your money or opportunity by force; Buffet has more likely enhanced your life by providing the necessary capital to companies that make products or provide services that you desire. The fact that Buffet is rich has no negative impact on your ability to accumulate wealth, and his success likely makes your ability to accumulate wealth more possible if you desire. But even if the wealth gap was a "bad" thing, the government has no standing to address the issue. Nonetheless, the government uses the tax code to redistribute wealth as a central theme of their activities. It is important that we citizens understand

and insist that the use of the taxing authority of the federal government is to fund those activities ceded to it by the states, most of which are in Article One Section 8.

These methods and arguments put forth by the anti-constitutionalist are to implement communism in one form or another. Let's now look at the ten tenets of communism as espoused by Marx (et al.). As we go through these tenets, we'll look back to the Constitution and see with more specificity why I say that communism is illegal in the United States. As a point of clarification, when I say that communism is illegal, I don't mean that you can't be a communist in the United States, which would be violative of the First Amendment's protection of freedom of speech. What I mean is that none of the principles of communism can be implemented without Constitutional amendment. As we go through these tenets, I think that you'll find it alarming how far we have already slid into a society that looks nothing like what the framers and founders envisioned. The breeziness with which the United States' marches toward some form of totalitarianism should be alarming to anyone reading this book. When will we ever hear in our media a serious discussion on what it means to be a socialist and what do the anti-constitutionalist candidates actually believe in and what do they think of these communist tenets and how do they plan on implementing their vision given the protections the people have from the government through our Constitution

Let's look at what communism really is from Karl Marx himself. Here are the ten tenets of Marxism

1. **Abolition of private property in land and application of all rents of land to public purpose.**[1] This one always makes me think of the movie Dr. Zhivago, when the "people" took the good Dr.'s family home at the beginning of the Russian Revolution in 1917. As almost always happens, the taking of liberties and implementation of totalitarianism starts slowly. In the United States, one way we see this happening with exorbitant property tax rates. In states with heavy property tax burdens close to half the value of your home will be paid to the government over the course of a 30-year mortgage. So the government won't take your actual property (unless you don't pay your property tax), but they will extract the value of your property over time. Even If you are fortunate enough to have no mortgage, you will be placed into serfdom as your overlords will continue to extract their pound of flesh from you for eternity. What's worse is that the bulk of your property taxes will go to fund salaries, pensions, and benefits for unaccountable, unionized public sector workers. Even when there is an economic downturn, and property values go down, the state will raise the mill rates to be sure they still take what they need from you.

When we look at this issue constitutionally, two different aspects of the above communist tenet regarding the taking of property are addressed. First, in Article One Section Eight, where tax receipts can only be used for the delineated authority consented to by the states, not for the unspecified public purpose advocated in the above tenet. We see more specific constitutional prohibition for this type of overreach by the state in the Fifth Amendment, it says:

; nor shall private property be taken for public use without just compensation.

There could not be a much clearer prohibition against such government overreach, but we need to remain vigilant in order to prevent ambitious anti-constitutionalists from overstepping their bounds. There is already one infamous case where the government took property from a citizen and gave it to another private-sector entity because it was supposedly in the public's interest.

2. A heavy progressive or graduated income tax.[2]

At the turn of the last century, progressives were successful in passing the Sixteenth Amendment to the Constitution establishing the federal government's authority to collect taxes on income. Since then, progressives have increasingly used the income tax as a method to redistribute wealth. While the process by which the government gained the authority to tax income is completely legitimate, what the government does with those receipts is not. I have no particular problem with an income tax that is somewhat progressive; however, an overly progressive tax is little more than punitive for the taxpayer while adversely affecting society in general by de-incenting those with higher incomes. Overly burdensome tax rates will stymy capital formation, and without capital formation, you will not have any innovation or competition. The laws of economics are like the laws of physics; you just can't get around them. Ask an anti-constitutionalist to explain capital formation in an environment that has marginal tax rates of ninety percent, and you'll see a confounded look on their faces. Again, Congress has the authority to tax, but it can only spend those dollars on the items enumerated in the Constitution.

3. Abolition of all rights of inheritance.[3]

For a group that claims not to like money communists sure want to get their hands on as much of it as possible. It's like N.Y. Mayor Bill Diblasio said, "there is plenty of money; it's just in the wrong hands." Communists and anti-constitutionalists see money the same way as they see guns, they don't want you to have any guns or money; they want to keep all of the guns and money to themselves, just like good totalitarians. So, if the federal government needed to amend the Constitution in order to tax your income wouldn't they then need to amend the Constitution to take your inheritance? Certainly. Only through gaining your consent through the amendment process could the government tax or take your inheritance. We occasionally hear about schemes where progressives are trying to get their hands on your inheritance, but now you know that they have no standing whatsoever on the issue. Remember too that the bulk of the money that you inherit has already been taxed.

4. Confiscation of the property of all emigrants and rebels.[4]

What's with communism and taking people's stuff? As is typical of progressives, they always accuse others of the shortcomings they themselves possess. Today's anti-constitutionalist is always accusing others of intolerance, well the communist is really the intolerant one. If you disagree with the regime to the point where you leave the country, the government will take all of your property, and if you stay in the country and do not conform then your property will be taken too. While we have not yet seen this in our country, we have seen increasingly politicized decisions to prosecute crimes. If you are one of them, you will be much more likely to get away with your transgression than if you are on the outside.

5. **Centralization of credit in the hands of the state, by means of a national bank with state capital and an exclusive monopoly.**[5]

Here we are again back to Money. The Constitution certainly does not bestow the authority for a monopoly on banking upon the federal government. As it pertains to money we find the government's role in Article One Section Eight, it simply says:

To coin Money, regulate the Value thereof, and of foreign Coin, and fix the Standard of Weights and Measures.

So, if the states consented to Congress having the authority to Coin and regulate the value of money, why is it that they outsourced that responsibility to the Federal Reserve? Unsurprisingly, in 1913 during the progressive movement Congress established the Federal Reserve Bank, as a private corporation, the shareholders of which are private banks. By establishing the Federal Reserve Bank, the government could now more directly control the actions of banks than the Constitution authorizes. It certainly seems that both the outsourcing of the constitutionally obligated role of coining and regulating the value of money and the outsourced firm (the Fed) having broader authority than the Constitution granted the government.

The pattern of Constitutional overreach remains the same as the anti-constitutionalists, past and present move us continually toward totalitarianism absent the consent of the governed. Unless the people call out our leaders for their actions, we will one day wake up in a completely unrecognizable place.

6. **Centralization of the means of communication and transportation in the hands of the state.**[6]

Boy, these guys like to control things. Of course, monopolistic state-run propaganda is always the goal of the totalitarian. The Constitution takes a position 180 degrees from this; it calls for a free press. Having a free press never used to be controversial. A free press was something that virtually everyone was in favor of, and it seems naturally American to hold this belief. The country's views too seem to be changing. The press has had an anti-constitutional bias for decades, but they now are completely out of the closet. While the "mainstream" media is not yet government controlled the issue of National Public Radio (NPR) for radio and the Public Broadcasting Service (PBS) for television is a different story. NPR and PBS are both publically (government) and privately funded. There is no provision to be found anywhere in the Constitution that allows for government involvement in the press, period. One more place where anti-constitutionalists have breached the high walls meant to ensure our liberty.

If we look at most of the country's other media outlets, we see disturbing trends. While the state does not own today's media, we see that there is such close coordination between most of the media and the and the democrat party that you are unable to tell where one ends, and the other begins.

7. **Extension of factories and instruments of production owned by the state; the bringing into cultivation of waste lands, and the improvement of the soil generally in accordance with a common plan.**[7] When people define communism, they often pull their definition from this tenet. They define communism as "the state controlling the means of production," communism is clearly more, but certainly, they want to control the means of production and everything else. The Constitution is clear on the federal governments' role in commerce; it says:

To regulate Commerce with foreign Nations, and among the several States, and with the Indian Tribes[8]

The "commerce clause," like the first amendment's recognition of a free press does the opposite of what the communist or anti-constitutionalist would like; it precludes government involvement in commerce. The Constitution's commerce clause was intended to simply ensure the free flow of commerce from state to state. The goal of having free trade *among* the states could not be more plain. Trade was the primary driver of the Annapolis Convention that directly led to the Constitutional Convention. Yet today we have legion upon legion of bureaucrats descending, not upon only the states, but directly regulating commerce within the corporations themselves. These bureaucratic regulations not only take the shape of rules that must be complied with, but with fines to be paid for non-compliance. Moreover, there are also fees (read as taxes) that these industries need to pay that are made up by the executive branch of government where Article One Section Eight says clearly that:

The Congress shall have Power To lay and collect Taxes, Duties, Imposts and Excises[9]

Why then are bureaucrats taxing? As with their typical strategy, the anti-constitutionalist will try to use the instrumentalities of government to get his desired result, or said differently; he'll use the law against you at the point of a gun. He understands that, right now, he can't own *the means of production,* but he has found a way, through complete distortion and abuse of our commerce clause to *control* the means of production.

Through rules on safety, the environment, labor, and others, there are almost no products available for purchase in the United States that are not regulated by the federal government in some fashion. Yet we constantly hear anti-constitutionalists talk about the dangers of the lack of regulation of some component of our society or other. In the United States, the government does not have the Constitutional authority to control the means of production either directly or through illegal manipulation of our commerce clause.

8. Equal obligation of all to work. Establishment of Industrial armies, especially for agriculture.[10]

This snapshot into the mind of the totalitarian communist is stark and grim. The *equal obligation of all to work* said differently is forced labor. So here is how communism really goes down for any Che Guevara T-shirt wearing readers. Communists (and anti-constitutionalists) hate the rich. Once the communist regime's ruling class steals money and property of the rich, the economy will fail, and the proletariat (the people) will be put to work to serve their new masters, not as employees, but as slaves. The screed put forth by the communist anti-constitutionalist about the one percent vs. the ninety-nine percent is never more true than in regimes adhering to this type of totalitarian society. In any, and every society, there is always the one percent, however in a communist regime (think North Korea) after the rich, there is only one class, the servants of the rich. It strikes me odd that those misguided anti-constitutionalists in our society who disparage "capitalism" (another Marx term) and who advocate for reparations for the wrongs of slavery are actually looking to drive us all back into slavery. This tenet brings home the true nature of communism more clearly than any of the others. Remember this when you next listen to Bernie Sanders or any of the other "democratic socialists."

9. **Combination of agriculture with manufacturing industries; gradual abolition of the distinction between town and country by a more equable distribution of the population over the country.**[11]

As long as you are being forced to work, you might as well be told where to live too. I say slightly tongue in cheek (and only slightly) that this is the type of thing the framers had in mind when they wrote the Ninth Amendment to the Constitution (just because we didn't list something as a right doesn't mean we aren't claiming it as one). Today in the United States we see an effort, not necessarily for the equal distribution of the population, but a drive to the concentration of people around cities and where there are population centers we see efforts to redistribute people so that there are no wealthy communities and no poor communities. I certainly don't have a problem with any good citizen who wants to move into my community; the government just has no standing to make me subsidize it. People who believe that they can force you to work and tell you where to live do not believe that they are your equal and don't believe that they have any desire to have your consent to their desires.

10. **Free education for all children in government schools. Abolition of children's factory labor in its present form. Combination of education with industrial production, etc. etc.**[12]

When the communist and the anti-constitutionalist talk about free government education, they are not giving you an option. Government education is compulsory; it is mandatory. I think it is more honest to call it government education and not "public" education. In our Constitution, there is no mention or implication of education. Education was meant to be *reserved to the states respectively, or to the people.* Why then do we have a Department of Education? Moreover, why do we fund academic institutions that blatantly denounce free speech? In the United States today, even in many of the communities that could clearly benefit most by parental choice in education, we see those efforts being undermined. If education is so important, and it is, why is it that my tax dollars will only fund government schools? The education system in today's America is little more than an indoctrination mill. The curriculum is put together by the anti-constitutionalist "elite" and taught by an overwhelmingly anti-constitutionalist faculty.

So those are the ten tenets of communism. Let me sum them up for you, but I only need three tenets to do so.

1. The government will take all forms of your property, including land, income and inheritance either directly or through taxation.
2. The government will run all banking, communications, education, and industry
3. The government will force you to work, tell you where to live and what to think

It is no wonder that the attempted implementation of communism has led to more misery and death than anything else in the history of mankind, go get 'em, Bernie.

These ten tenets of communism are aggressively infiltrating our republic. The methodology by which the tenets are being introduced was first brought to light in the 1958 book "The Naked Communist" by W. Cleon Skousen, a former FBI agent, and political philosopher. While the book originally suggested that the now-defunct Soviet Union was behind the scheme, the fact remains that the methodology has been startlingly successful. I have listed the 45 steps outlined in Skousen's book, and while some are now outdated given the collapse of the Soviet Union, the general concepts remain intact.

The 45 steps, like the ten tenets of communism, are frighteningly totalitarian and have no respect for the individual. The forty-five steps can be broken down into 10 categories

1. Discredit the American founding
2. Cede U.S. authority to a central world power (The United Nations)
3. Accept, as opposed to resisting, communist aggression
4. Recognizing communism as legitimate
5. Financially support communist regimes
6. Infiltrate U.S. institutions, political parties, education, media, business and unions
7. Put the state above family
8. Take over social institutions and psychiatry
9. Replace religion with the State
10. Debase U.S. culture

1. U.S. should accept coexistence as the only alternative to atomic war.

2. U.S. should be willing to capitulate in preference to engaging in atomic war

3. Develop the illusion that total disarmament by the U.S. would be a demonstration of "moral strength."

4. Permit free trade between all nations regardless of Communist affiliation and regardless of whether or not items could be used for war

5. Extend long term loans to Russia and Soviet satellites.

6. Provide American aid to all nations regardless of Communist domination.

7. Grant recognition of Red China and admission of Red China to the U.N.

8. Set up East and West Germany as separate states in spite of Khrushchev's promise in 1955 to settle the Germany question by free elections under supervision of the U.N.

9. Prolong the conferences to ban atomic tests because the U.S. has agreed to suspend tests as long as negotiations are in progress.

10. Allow all Soviet satellites individual representation in the U.N.

11. Promote the U.N. as the only hope for mankind. If its charter is rewritten, demand that it be set up as a one world government with its own independent armed forces.

12. Resist any attempt to outlaw the Communist Party.

13. Do away with loyalty oaths.

14. Continue giving Russia access to the U.S. Patent Office.

15. Capture one or both of the political parties in the U.S.

16. Use technical decisions of the courts to weaken basic American institutions, by claiming their activities violate civil rights.

17. Get control of the schools. Use them as transmission belts for Socialism and current Communist propaganda. Soften the curriculum. Get control of teachers associations. Put the party line in textbooks.

18. Gain control of all student newspapers.

19. Use student riots to foment public protests against programs or organizations that are under Communist attack.

20. Infiltrate the press. Get control of book review assignments, editorial writing, policy making positions.

21. Gain control of key positions in radio, T.V. & motion pictures.

22. Continue discrediting American culture by degrading all form of artistic expression. An American Communist cell was told to "eliminate all good sculpture from parks and buildings," substituting shapeless, awkward and meaningless forms.

23. Control art critics and directors of art museums. "Our plan is to promote ugliness, repulsive, meaningless art."

24. Eliminate all laws governing obscenity by calling them "censorship" and a violation of free speech and free press.

25. Break down cultural standards of morality by promoting pornography and obscenity in books, magazines, motion pictures, radio and T.V.

26. Present homosexuality, degeneracy and promiscuity as "normal, natural and healthy."

27. Infiltrate the churches and replace revealed religion with "social" religion. Discredit the Bible and emphasize the need for intellectual maturity, which does not need a "religious crutch."

28. Eliminate prayer or any phase of religious expression in the schools on the grounds that it violates the principle of "separation of church and state"

29. Discredit the American Constitution by calling it inadequate, old fashioned, out of step with modern needs, a hindrance to cooperation between nations on a worldwide basis.

30. Discredit the American founding fathers. Present them as selfish aristocrats who had no concern for the "common man."

31. Belittle all forms of American culture and discourage the teaching of American history on the ground that it was only a minor part of "the big picture." Give more emphasis to Russian history since the Communists took over.

32. Support any socialist movement to give centralized control over any

part of the culture education, social agencies, welfare programs, mental health clinics, etc.

33. Eliminate all laws or procedures which interfere with the operation of the Communist apparatus.

34. Eliminate the House Committee on Un-American Activities.

35. Discredit and eventually dismantle the FBI.

36. Infiltrate and gain control of more unions.

37. Infiltrate and gain control of big business.

38. Transfer some of the powers of arrest from the police to social agencies. Treat all behavioral problems as psychiatric disorders which no one but psychiatrists can understand or treat.

39. Dominate the psychiatric profession and use mental health laws as a means of gaining coercive control over those who oppose communist goals.

40. Discredit the family as an institution. Encourage promiscuity and easy divorce.

41. Emphasize the need to raise children away from the negative influence of parents. Attribute prejudices, mental blocks, and retarding of children to suppressive influence of parents.

42. Create the impression that violence and insurrection are legitimate aspects of the American tradition; that students and special interest groups should rise up and make a "united force" to solve economic, political or social problems.

43. Overthrow all colonial governments before native populations are ready for self-government.

44. Internationalize the Panama Canal.

45. Repeal the Connally Reservation so the U.S. cannot prevent the World Court from seizing jurisdiction over domestic problems. Give the World Court jurisdiction over domestic problems. Give the World Court jurisdiction over nations and individuals alike[13]

To anyone willing to look, these steps have been central to the attempts to undermine the United States for decades. Today's anti-constitutionalist communist uses another obvious power grab by creating climate change alarmism. The federal government has no role in climate change, irrespective of your views on whether or not the climate is changing, and if the climate is changing, what role has man had in that change. Let's look at the some of what is in the Green New Deal and see that a government moored to the Constitution would need to be amended prior to implementation. We'll also see that the Green New Deal is nothing more than a Marxist, totalitarian power grab

1. *Guaranteeing a job with a family-sustaining wage, adequate family and medical leave, paid vacations, and retirement security to all people of the United States."[14]*

So the Green New Deal starts with economic redistribution in which the government has no standing. Flat out Marxism. The Constitution will need amending to accomplish this legitimately.

2. *Providing all people of the United States with — (i) high-quality health care; (ii) affordable, safe, and adequate housing; (iii) economic security; and (iv) access to clean water, clean air, healthy and affordable food, and nature."[15]*

Health care, housing, economic security, and food; this is how hundreds of millions of individuals have been killed by communism in the past hundred, or so, years. When will we get to the climate? The Constitution will need amending to accomplish this legitimately.

3. *Providing resources, training, and high-quality education, including higher education, to all people of the United States."* [16]

Free education. The federal government has no standing in education. The Constitution will need amending to accomplish this legitimately.

4. *Meeting 100 percent of the power demand in the United States through clean, renewable, and zero-emission energy sources."* [17]

The federal government has no standing in energy. The Constitution will need amending to accomplish this legitimately.

5. *Repairing and upgrading the infrastructure in the United States by eliminating pollution and greenhouse gas emissions as much as technologically feasible."* [18]

The federal government has no standing in repairing infrastructure in the states. The Constitution will need amending to accomplish this legitimately.

6. *Building or upgrading to energy-efficient, distributed, and 'smart' power grids and working to ensure affordable access to electricity."* [19]

The federal government has no standing in building electric energy infrastructure. The Constitution will need amending to accomplish this legitimately.

7. *Upgrading all existing buildings in the United States and building new buildings to achieve maximal energy efficiency, water efficiency, safety, affordability, comfort, and durability, including through electrification."[20]*

Really? The federal government has no standing in any private property in the United States. The Constitution will need amending to accomplish this legitimately.

8. *Overhauling transportation systems in the United States to eliminate pollution and greenhouse gas emissions from the transportation sector as much as is technologically feasible, including through investment in — (i) zero-emission vehicle infrastructure and manufacturing; (ii) clean, affordable, and accessible public transportation; and (iii) high-speed rail."[21]*

The federal government has no standing in telling citizens how they are to travel nor investing in the means of transportation. The Constitution will need amending to accomplish this legitimately.

9. *Spurring massive growth in clean manufacturing in the United States and removing pollution and greenhouse gas emissions from manufacturing and industry as much as is technologically feasible." [22]*

The federal government has no standing in education. The Constitution will need amending to accomplish this legitimately.

10. *Working collaboratively with farmers and ranchers in the United States to eliminate pollution and greenhouse gas*

emissions from the agricultural sector as much as is technologically feasible."[23]

The Federal government has no standing in agriculture. The Constitution will need amending to accomplish this legitimately.

As could be expected, the Green New Deal is little more than a totalitarian power grab. The federal government has no standing in anything that is being proposed. When viewed in light of the tenets of communism and the 45 steps they have embarked upon to implement communism, the Green New Deal completely comports with communist ideology. The extensive and fawning media coverage has again completely failed the American people. The media asked some questions about the cost of this undertaking, but, there were no questions about the government's role in the scheme. It falls to the American people to raise the questions and insist that we consent to any additional power ceded to the federal government.

CHAPTER 17:

SO WHAT?

I hope that you were able to stick with me through this book and that I have made a compelling case for an originalist interpretation of the Constitutional. Hopefully important insight has been gained that even though the originalist does not believe that the 14th amendment's equal protection clause provides for anything other than the issues around citizenship for former slaves it does not mean that the originalist does not believe that others could also be entitled to specific enumeration of rights, but that too would require amendment or said more plainly, consent of the governed. And if it is so obvious that other "special classes" are so entitled couldn't they too easily make it through the amendment process and avoid the dangers of the tyranny of the majority or judicial and executive legislating?

However, I believe America will be much better off if we simply recognize all of our God-given unalienable rights in one another as individuals and not part of separate classes. I believe in the greater macro that all men are created equal under God and the law and to approach citizens as citizens (yes citizens) and as individuals as opposed to members of an aggrieved (or allegedly aggrieved) class is the surest way to put us all on equal footing.

If nothing else I hope your takeaway is that from the Annapolis Convention, through Philadelphia and all of the Constitutional amendments thereafter that one thing remained constant in holding our republic together until Franklin Roosevelt's New Deal; that the Consent of the Governed was always sought to change or expand the power of the central government, and until we re-claim that notion and demand it from government we will be adrift as a republic.

We as a citizenry need to have, at least a working knowledge of our civics and Constitution and at every single turn challenge those in power as to where exactly and precisely and by what means they believe that they or the government has standing in whatever issue they are claiming jurisdiction over. Most often, their answer will be unconstitutionally unsatisfactory to anyone with an originalist and knowledgeable perspective.

While I have not touched on race specifically in this book, I earnestly believe that Constitutional originalism and the mindset that accompanies it is the best remedy for any racial tensions that may exist. If we all take one another at face value as individuals with a divine spark, granted to you by our Creator with certain unalienable rights would not we all move closer together as a species? We must resist attempts by the mal-intentioned to balkanize us.

As we move to another election cycle (as it seems we are always in) we need to be especially vigilant in the not letting politicians and media figures alike, control the language and define us inaccurately and maliciously. While the Democrats are flat-out communists and their proposals, as discussed above, are clearly unconstitutional so too do the Republicans offer up programs that have no constitutional basis.

Furthermore, by understanding our founding and the framing of our Constitution, we can learn the 'tricks' of the despot. We know that his reliance upon clauses such as Article One's Taxing and Necessary and Proper clauses are red herrings for totalitarianism.

Know too that our magnificent Constitution did not cause our County's most egregious ills, they were cured through it.

This is your Constitution, don't let anyone take it away from you.

SOURCE NOTES

Introduction
  1. "Perspectives on the Constitution: A republic if you can keep it". Constitutioncenter.org

Chapter 2.
  1. "Lee Resolution". Constitution.com
  2. "The Declaration of Independence: A Transcription". Archives.gov
  3. "The Declaration of Independence: A Transcription". Archives.gov
  4. "The Declaration of Independence: A Transcription". Archives.gov
  5. "The Declaration of Independence: A Transcription". Archives.gov

Chapter 3.
  1. "Lee Resolution". Constitution.com
  2. "The Constitution of the United States: A Transcription". Archives.gov

Chapter 4.
  1. "The Constitution of the United States: A Transcription". Archives.gov

Chapter 5.

1. "The Constitution of the United States: A Transcription". Archives.gov

2. "The Declaration of Independence: A Transcription". Archives.gov

3. "The Constitution of the United States: A Transcription". Archives.gov

4. "The Constitution of the United States: A Transcription". Archives.gov

5. "The Constitution of the United States: A Transcription". Archives.gov

6. "The Declaration of Independence: A Transcription". Archives.gov

7. "The Constitution of the United States: A Transcription". Archives.gov

8. "The Constitution of the United States: A Transcription". Archives.gov

9. "The Constitution of the United States: A Transcription". Archives.gov

10. "Unsustainable, Unconstitutional General Welfare Spending". Humanevents.com

11. "The Constitution of the United States: A Transcription". Archives.gov

12. "The Constitution of the United States: A Transcription". Archives.gov

Chapter 6.
1. "The Constitution of the United States: A Transcription". Archives.gov
2. "The Constitution of the United States: A Transcription". Archives.gov
3. "The Constitution of the United States: A Transcription". Archives.gov

Chapter 7.
1. "The Declaration of Independence: A Transcription". Archives.gov
2. "The Constitution of the United States: A Transcription". Archives.gov
3. "The Constitution of the United States: A Transcription". Archives.gov

Chapter 8.
1. "The Declaration of Independence: A Transcription". Archives.gov

Chapter 9.
1. "The Founders on a Living Constitution". Whatwouldthefoundersthink.com
2. "The Founders on a Living Constitution". Whatwouldthefoundersthink.com
3. "From James Madison to Henry Lee 25 June 1824". Founders.archives.gov
4. "The Declaration of Independence: A Transcription". Archives.gov
5. "Thomas Jefferson: Founding Fathers Quotes". Foundingfathersquotes.com

6. "Thomas Jefferson, All powers not Delegated are reserved to the People". The federalistpapers.org
7. "From Thomas Jefferson to William Johnson 12 June 1823". Founders.archives.gov

Chapter 10.
1. "The Constitution of the United States: A Transcription". Archives.gov

Chapter 11.
1. "The Bill of Rights: A Transcription". Archives.gov
2. "The Bill of Rights: A Transcription". Archives.gov
3. "The Bill of Rights: A Transcription". Archives.gov
4. "The Bill of Rights: A Transcription". Archives.gov
5. "The Bill of Rights: A Transcription". Archives.gov
6. "The Bill of Rights: A Transcription". Archives.gov
7. "The Bill of Rights: A Transcription". Archives.gov
8. "The Founding Fathers Explain the Second Amendment, This Says it all". Thefederalistpapers.org
9. "The Constitutions of all of our States assert that all Power is Inherent in the People". Foundersquotes.com
10. "The Founding Fathers Explain the Second Amendment, This Says it all".Thefederalistpapers.org
11. "The Founding Fathers Explain the Second Amendment, This Says it all".Thefederalistpapers.org
12. "The Founding Fathers Explain the Second Amendment, This Says it all".Thefederalistpapers.org
13. "A Strong Body Makes The Mind Strong, As to the Species of Exercise I Advise the Gun". Foundersquotes.com
14. "The Founding Fathers Explain the Second Amendment, This Says it all".Thefederalistpapers.org

15. "The Founding Fathers Explain the Second Amendment, This Says it all".Thefederalistpapers.org

16. "Alexander Hamilton, Federalist Paper #28 On the Power of the People to Keep the Government in Check". Thefederalistpapers.org

17. "The Founding Fathers Explain the Second Amendment, This Says it all".Thefederalistpapers.org

18. "Benjamin Franklin on Safety and Liberty". Thefederalistpapers.org

19. "The Declaration of Independence: A Transcription". Archives.gov

20. "The Bill of Rights: A Transcription". Archives.gov

21. "The Bill of Rights: A Transcription". Archives.gov

22. "John Adams to Abigail Adams, 3 July 1776". Founders. archives.gov

23. "The Bill of Rights: A Transcription". Archives.gov

24. "The Declaration of Independence: A Transcription". Archives.gov

25. "For the National Gazette 27 March 1792". Founders. archives.gov

26. "James Madison Quote, Charity". Thefederalistpapers.org

27. "Santo Domingo Refugees, 10 January 1794" Founders. archives.org

28. "Nine Quotes from the Founders about Economics, Capitalism and Banking". Thefederalistpapers.org

29. "Nine Quotes from the Founders about Economics, Capitalism and Banking". Thefederalistpapers.org

30. "The General Welfare Clause" the "Commerce Clause" and MussoliniCare". Renewamerica.com

31. "Ben Franklin, The Best Way to Help the Poor". Thefederalistpapers.org

32. "Ben Franklin on Liberty". Mises.org

33. "Voting for Dollars". Americanthinker.com
34. "The Bill of Rights: A Transcription". Archives.gov
35. "The Declaration of Independence: A Transcription". Archives.gov
36. "The Declaration of Independence: A Transcription". Archives.gov
37. "The Bill of Rights: A Transcription". Archives.gov
38. "The Bill of Rights: A Transcription". Archives.gov
39. "The Bill of Rights: A Transcription". Archives.gov
40. "The Bill of Rights: A Transcription". Archives.gov

Chapter 12.
1. "Mussolini's Ideas of the State and its American Defenders". Mises.org

Chapter 13.
1. "13th Amendment to the U.S. Constitution, The Abolition of Slavery". Archives.gov
2. "13th Amendment to the U.S. Constitution, The Abolition of Slavery". Archives.gov
3. "The Constitution: Amendments 11-27". Archives.gov
4. "The Constitution: Amendments 11-27". Archives.gov
5. "The Constitution: Amendments 11-27". Archives.gov

Chapter 14.
1. "The Constitution: Amendments 11-27". Archives.gov
2. "The Constitution: Amendments 11-27". Archives.gov

Chapter 15.
1. "To James Madison from Thomas Jefferson 20 December 1787". Founders.achives.gov

Chapter 16.

1. "The Ten Planks of the Communist Manifesto 1848 by Karl Heinrich Marx". Laissez-fairerepublic.com

2. "The Ten Planks of the Communist Manifesto 1848 by Karl Heinrich Marx". Laissez-fairerepublic.com

3. "The Ten Planks of the Communist Manifesto 1848 by Karl Heinrich Marx". Laissez-fairerepublic.com

4. "The Ten Planks of the Communist Manifesto 1848 by Karl Heinrich Marx". Laissez-fairerepublic.com

5. "The Ten Planks of the Communist Manifesto 1848 by Karl Heinrich Marx". Laissez-fairerepublic.com

6. "The Ten Planks of the Communist Manifesto 1848 by Karl Heinrich Marx". Laissez-fairerepublic.com

7. "The Ten Planks of the Communist Manifesto 1848 by Karl Heinrich Marx". Laissez-fairerepublic.com

8. "The Constitution of the United States: A Transcription". Archives.gov

9. "The Constitution of the United States: A Transcription". Archives.gov

10. "The Ten Planks of the Communist Manifesto 1848 by Karl Heinrich Marx". Laissez-fairerepublic.com

11. "The Ten Planks of the Communist Manifesto 1848 by Karl Heinrich Marx". Laissez-fairerepublic.com

12. "The Ten Planks of the Communist Manifesto 1848 by Karl Heinrich Marx". Laissez-fairerepublic.com

13. "Naked Communist and Capitalist Archive by W. CLEON SKOUSEN–FBI Whistleblower". Archive.org

14. "H-Res 109 116th Congress 2019-2020". Congress.gov

15. "H-Res 109 116th Congress 2019-2020". Congress.gov

16. "H-Res 109 116th Congress 2019-2020". Congress.gov

17. "H-Res 109 116th Congress 2019-2020". Congress.gov

18. "H-Res 109 116th Congress 2019-2020". Congress.gov

19. "H-Res 109 116th Congress 2019-2020". Congress.gov
20. "H-Res 109 116th Congress 2019-2020". Congress.gov
21. "H-Res 109 116th Congress 2019-2020". Congress.gov
22. "H-Res 109 116th Congress 2019-2020". Congress.gov
23. "H-Res 109 116th Congress 2019-2020". Congress.gov